Rodin User's Handbook

Covers Rodin v.2.8

Rodin User's Handbook

Contents

Contents   1

Preface   5

Foreword   7

1   Introduction   9
   1.1   Overview 9
      1.1.1   Formats of this Handbook 10
      1.1.2   Rodin Wiki 10
      1.1.3   Contributing 10
   1.2   Further Reading 10
      1.2.1   Modeling in Event-B: System and Software Engineering, J.-R. Abrial (2010) 10
      1.2.2   Rodin: An Open Toolset for Modelling and Reasoning in Event-B (2009) 11
      1.2.3   The B-Method, an Introduction (Steve Schneider) 11
      1.2.4   Event-B Cookbook 11
      1.2.5   Proofs for the Working Engineer (2008) 11
      1.2.6   The Proof Obligation Generator (2005) 12
   1.3   Conventions 12
   1.4   Acknowledgements 12
   1.5   DEPLOY 13
   1.6   Creative Commons Legal Code 13

2   Tutorial   15
   2.1   Outline 15
   2.2   Before Getting Started 16
      2.2.1   Systems Development 17
      2.2.2   Formal Modelling 17
      2.2.3   Predicate Logic 17
      2.2.4   Event-B 18
      2.2.5   Rodin 18
      2.2.6   Eclipse 18

2.3	Installation	18
	2.3.1 Install Rodin for the first time	19
	2.3.2 Install new plugins	21
2.4	The First Machine: A Traffic Light Controller	21
	2.4.1 Excursus: The specification process	23
	2.4.2 Project Setup	24
	2.4.3 Camille, a text-based editor	26
	2.4.4 Building the Model	26
	2.4.5 The Final Traffic Light Model	31
2.5	Mathematical notation	32
	2.5.1 Predicates	33
	2.5.2 Data types	34
	2.5.3 Operations on Sets	35
	2.5.4 Introducing user-defined types	36
	2.5.5 Relations	36
	2.5.6 Arithmetic	37
2.6	Introducing Contexts	37
	2.6.1 Create a Context	38
	2.6.2 Populate the Context	38
	2.6.3 The Final Context	42
2.7	Event-B Concepts	43
	2.7.1 Contexts	43
	2.7.2 Machines	44
	2.7.3 Events	44
	2.7.4 Refinement	45
2.8	Contexts and Refinement	47
	2.8.1 Data Refinement	47
	2.8.2 A Context with Colours	48
	2.8.3 The Actual Data Refinement	49
	2.8.4 The refined machine with data refinement for peds_go . .	51
	2.8.5 Witnesses	52
	2.8.6 Discussion	54
	2.8.7 The Refined Machine with All Data Refinement	54
	2.8.8 One more Refinement: The Push Button	55
	2.8.9 Discussion	57
2.9	Proving	57
	2.9.1 The Celebrity Problem	57
	2.9.2 Importing a project	58
	2.9.3 Fixing Problems	59
	2.9.4 The Final Second Refinement	60
	2.9.5 The Celebrity algorithm	61
	2.9.6 The First Proof	63
	2.9.7 Proving — an Art or a Science?	68
2.10	Proving Deadlock Freeness	69
	2.10.1 Deadlock Freeness of initial model	69
	2.10.2 Deadlock Freeness of First Refinement	75

2.11 Outlook 80

3 Reference   **81**
  3.1 The Rodin Platform 81
      3.1.1 Eclipse in General 81
      3.1.2 The Event-B Perspective 83
      3.1.3 Customizing a perspective suitable for RODIN 86
      3.1.4 The Event-B Editor 88
      3.1.5 The Structural Event-B Editor 89
      3.1.6 Wizards 94
      3.1.7 The Proving Perspective 99
      3.1.8 Preferences 111
  3.2 Event-B's modelling notation 121
      3.2.1 About the notation that we use 121
      3.2.2 Substitutions 122
      3.2.3 Contexts 122
      3.2.4 Machines 123
      3.2.5 Well-definedness proof obligations 131
      3.2.6 Theorems 132
      3.2.7 Generated proof obligations 133
      3.2.8 Visibility of identifiers 133
  3.3 Mathematical Notation 135
      3.3.1 Introduction 135
      3.3.2 Predicates 138
      3.3.3 Booleans 140
      3.3.4 Sets 140
      3.3.5 Relations 145
      3.3.6 Arithmetic 151
      3.3.7 Typing 152
      3.3.8 Assignments 153
  3.4 Proving 156
      3.4.1 Sequents 156
      3.4.2 Proof Rules 156
      3.4.3 Proof Tactics 158
      3.4.4 Provers 159
      3.4.5 How to Use the Provers Effectively 161
      3.4.6 Reasoners 162
      3.4.7 Purging Proofs 163
      3.4.8 Simplifying Proofs 164

4 Frequently Asked Questions   **167**
  4.1 General Questions 167
      4.1.1 Where can I get help? 167
      4.1.2 What is Event-B? 167
      4.1.3 What is the difference between Event-B and the B method?167
      4.1.4 What is Rodin? 168

	4.1.5	Where does the Rodin name come from?	168
	4.1.6	Where I can download Rodin?	168
	4.1.7	How to contribute and develop?	168
	4.1.8	My operating system is not supported! How can I install Rodin on my platform?	168
4.2		General Tool Usage	169
	4.2.1	Do I lose my proofs when I clean a project?	169
	4.2.2	How do I install external plugins without using the Eclipse Update Manager?	169
	4.2.3	The builder takes too long	169
	4.2.4	What are the ASCII shortcuts for mathematical operators?	170
	4.2.5	Pretty Print does not work on Linux	170
	4.2.6	Some mathematical characters are wrong	170
	4.2.7	No More Handles	170
	4.2.8	Software installation fails	170
	4.2.9	How do I send a bug report?	171
	4.2.10	Where did the GUI window go?	171
	4.2.11	Where vs. When: What's going on?	172
4.3		Modelling	172
	4.3.1	Witness for Xyz missing. Default witness generated	172
	4.3.2	Identifier Xyz should not occur free in a witness	172
	4.3.3	Witness Xyz must be a disappearing abstract variable or parameter in the INITIALISATION event	172
	4.3.4	I've added a witness for Xyz but it keeps saying "Identifier Xyz has not been defined"	172
	4.3.5	How can I create a new Event-B Project?	173
	4.3.6	How can I remove a Event-B Project?	173
	4.3.7	How can I export an Event-B Project?	173
	4.3.8	How can I import a Event-B Project?	174
	4.3.9	How can I change the name of a Event-B Project?	174
	4.3.10	How can I create a Event-B Component?	174
	4.3.11	How can I remove a Event-B Component?	174
	4.3.12	In the new Rodin Editor, how can I add an element to machine?	175
	4.3.13	How can I use multiple lines for a comment, predicate or expression (using the new editor)?	175
	4.3.14	How can I save a Context or a Machine?	175
4.4		Proving	176
	4.4.1	Help! Proving is difficult!	176
	4.4.2	How can I do a Proof by Induction?	176
	4.4.3	What do the labels on the proof tree mean?	176
Index			**177**

Preface

Nobody likes to write documentation, yet everybody agrees that documentation is crucially important. For a tool platform as complex as Rodin, documentation is necessary if it is supposed to succeed in reaching a wider audience.

The executive team of the DEPLOY project recognized this. In a meeting at ETH in 2010, the team established, amongst other things, that "it is clear that the current documentation would not support, say, an engineer in an automotive company to start using the tools without significant support". It then commissioned the creation of better Rodin documentation. This handbook is the result of this effort.

Rather than reinventing the wheel, we took all the existing documentation into account, restructured it, extended it where necessary, created plenty of cross-references, and put the resulting document through an editorial process to ensure readability.

A word of warning and encouragement: Don't expect to be an expert in Event-B modelling after reading this handbook. Its aim is to provide support while getting acquainted with the tool platform. It provides the basics of modelling and can also be used as a companion guide for experts. Beginners can work their way through the tutorial, which starts with installation and ends with moderately difficult proofs. Additional support is available in the form of an FAQ and a comprehensive index. Advanced users can refer to the comprehensive reference section, where they can quickly find essential information regarding the different formalisms.

Whenever the handbook requires former knowledge, it provides links and hints about where to get it. Whenever it stops, it provides references for further reading. In particular, it provides plenty of references to the Rodin Wiki, and provides information on how to get in touch with the Rodin community. We are confident that this handbook will achieve its mission to get new users acquainted with Rodin without frustration and hopefully some with fun.

Michael Jastram, Düsseldorf, 2012

6

Foreword

The Rodin tool supports the application of the Event-B formal method. It provides core functionality for syntactic analysis and proof-based verification of Event-B models. Rodin also provides extension points for a range of additional plug-ins that enrich the core functionality through support for features such as model checking, model animation, graphical front ends, additional proof capabilities and code generation. While the B Method, developed by Jean-Raymond Abrial in the early 1990s, is focused on supporting formal development of *software*, Event-B broadens the perspective to cover *systems*; instead of just modelling software components, Event-B is intended for modelling and reasoning about systems that may consist of physical components, electronics and software. An essential difference between Event-B and the B Method is that Event-B admits a richer notion of refinement in which new observables may be introduced in refinement steps; this means that complex interactions between subcomponents may be abstracted from in early stage modelling and then introduced through refinement in incremental stages.

At around the same time that Jean-Raymond was developing the concepts in Event-B, I was involved in an initiative with the University of Newcastle (Alexander Romanovsky, Cliff Jones), Åbo Akademi (Kaisa Sere, Elena Troubitsyna) and Jean-Raymond to put together an EU proposal on formal methods for dependable systems. That became the RODIN project (2004 to 2007) and a key part of the project was the development of an open source extensible toolset to support refinement-based formal development. Many of Jean-Raymond's ideas on Event-B were worked into the requirements for the tool and the development of the core tool platform was led by Jean-Raymond and Laurent Voisin (both then at ETH Zurich). Thorough analysis was undertaken to determine that Eclipse was the right platform on which to build an open toolset. The ease with which the core may be extended with plug-ins from a range of teams to provide seamless functionality indicates this was a good decision. The tools developed in the RODIN project took on the name of the project and, since it had a certain cachet, it was decided to retain the Rodin name for the tool after the project ended.

The RODIN Project was followed by the DEPLOY Project which addressed further development of the Rodin core and associated plug-ins in parallel with industrial-scale deployment of the Rodin tools. Exposing the tools to serious industrial users in DEPLOY drove the developers to implement significant improvements in performance, usability and stability of Rodin and key plug-ins such as ProB, the Theory plug-in, Camille and UML-B. Of course, as well as demanding improvements to the tool, the industrial users demanded documentation on the tool, which led to this handbook. Michael Jastram and the team at Düsseldorf have done an excellent job in pulling together, extending and improving various sources of documentation on the Rodin tool. Like the Rodin tools, it will serve as a valuable resource that will continue to evolve beyond the DEPLOY project.

Michael Butler, Southampton, 2012

Chapter 1

Introduction

This handbook provides documentation for users of the Rodin toolset, which provides tools for working with Event-B models.

Event-B is a formal method for system-level modelling and analysis. Key features of Event-B are the use of set theory as a modelling notation, the use of refinement to represent systems at different abstraction levels and the use of mathematical proof to verify consistency between refinement levels.

The Rodin Platform is an Eclipse-based IDE for Event-B that provides effective support for refinement and mathematical proof. The platform is open source, contributes to the Eclipse framework and is further extensible with plugins.

This handbook covers the use of the core platform. Documentation for developers and regarding extensions can be found in the Rodin wiki (1.1.2).

1.1 Overview

This handbook consists of five parts:

Introduction (Chapter 1) You are reading the introduction right now. Its purpose is to help you orient yourself and to find information quickly.

Tutorial (Chapter 2) If you are completely new to Rodin, the tutorial is a good way to get up to speed quickly. It guides you through the installation and usage of the tool and gives you an overview of the Event-B modelling notation.

Reference (Chapter 3) The reference section provides comprehensive documentation of Rodin and its components.

Frequently Asked Questions (Chapter 4) Common issues are listed by category in the FAQ.

Index We included an index particularly for the print version of the handbook, but it may be useful in the electronic versions as well.

1.1.1   Formats of this Handbook

The handbook comes in various formats:

Eclipse Help The Rodin Handbook is shipped with Rodin and can be accessed through the help system. The handbook will be updated with the standard Rodin update mechanism.

Online Help You can access the handbook online at `http://handbook.event-b.org`.

PDF Help Both online versions also include a link to the PDF version of the handbook.

1.1.2   Rodin Wiki

This handbook is complemented by the Rodin wiki (`http://wiki.event-b.org/`). Sometimes, the handbook will refer to the wiki for more information. Also, plugin and developer information is usually located in the wiki.

1.1.3   Contributing

The handbook is stored in the Rodin SVN repository and is authored in LaTeX. Changes that are checked in will be built automatically on the Jenkins server, managed by the University of Düsseldorf. The result should be available at `http://handbook.event-b.org` shortly after committing changes.

Each page of the online version also has a feedback button, where feedback can be left using an online form. This feedback will be processed on a regular basis by volunteers.

There is also a mailing list for handbook authors at `rodin-b-sharp-handbook@lists.sourceforge.net`.

You can also submit feedback via email to `rodin-handbook@formalmind.com`.

1.2   Further Reading

In this section, we present a selected list of reading materials that provide information that is not covered in this handbook.

1.2.1   Modeling in Event-B: System and Software Engineering, J.-R. Abrial (2010)

This book represents the ultimate authority on Event-B, written by its creator. The example from Section 2.10 is based on an example from the book.

From the editor: "A practical text suitable for an introductory or advanced course in formal methods, this book presents a mathematical approach to modelling and designing systems using an extension of the B formal method: Event-B. Based on the idea of refinement, the author's systematic approach allows the user to construct models gradually and to facilitate a systematic reasoning method by means of proofs. Readers will learn how to build models of programs and, more generally, discrete systems, but this is all done with practice in mind. The numerous examples provided arise from various sources of computer system developments, including sequential programs, concurrent programs and electronic circuits. The book also contains a large number of exercises and projects ranging in difficulty. Each of the examples included in the book has been proved using the Rodin Platform tool set, which is available free for download at www.event-b.org."

1.2.2 Rodin: An Open Toolset for Modelling and Reasoning in Event-B (2009)

This article discusses the design principles of the Rodin platform and the Event-B language and explains the motivation behind it.

The abstract states: "[...] we present the Rodin modelling tool that seamlessly integrates modelling and proving. We outline how the Event-B language was designed to facilitate proof and how the tool has been designed to support changes to models while minimising the impact of changes on existing proofs. We outline the important features of the prover architecture and explain how well-definedness is treated. [...]"

The authors J.-R. Abrial, M. Butler, S. Hallerstede, T. S. Hoang, F. Mehta and L. Voisin have published the article in the journal Software Tools and Technology Transfer (STTT).

1.2.3 The B-Method, an Introduction (Steve Schneider)

This text represents the "standard textbook" for learning formal modeling in B (rather than Event-B). As Event-B is similar to B, this book is a great introduction to the topic, allowing students to get acquainted with the subject matter, even without an instructor. (ISBN: 978-0333792841)

1.2.4 Event-B Cookbook

Those interested in more general guidelines on how to develop and structure formal models in Event-B, the paper "Towards a Cookbook for Modelling and Refinement of Control Problems"[1] may be of interest. It is an "attempt to develop some guidelines on modelling control problems in Event-B".

1.2.5 Proofs for the Working Engineer (2008)

In his dissertation at the ETH Zurich Fahrad Mehta describes how theorem proving can be a practical tool for software engineers and presents the ideas that are used in building Rodin's infrastructure.

---

[1]http://deploy-eprints.ecs.soton.ac.uk/108/

1.2.6   The Proof Obligation Generator (2005)

In this technical report (ETH Zürich) Stefan Hallerstede describes which proof obligations (see Section 3.2.7) are generated for a model and gives a justification why these are correct.

1.3   Conventions

We use the following conventions in this manual:

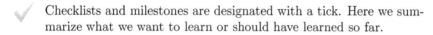 Checklists and milestones are designated with a tick. Here we summarize what we want to learn or should have learned so far.

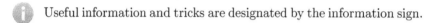 Useful information and tricks are designated by the information sign.

Potential problems and warnings are designated by a warning sign.

 Examples and Code are designated by a pencil.

We use `typewriter` font for file names and directories.

We use sans serif font for GUI elements like menus and buttons. Menu actions are depicted by a chain of elements, separated by "⟩", e.g. File ⟩ New ⟩ Event-B Component.

1.4   Acknowledgements

The content of this handbook has been growing since the formation of the European Union IST Project RODIN in 2004. Giving credit to every contributor is almost impossible and attempting to do so would almost certainly omit some people, which would contradict the spirit of this work. It should be sufficient to say that we extend our gratitude to all contributors to the Rodin Wiki (1.1.2). In particular, we would like to thank Systerel[2] for their significant contributions to the handbook as they have been the main driver behind the tool and its documentation.

Jean-Raymond Abrial and the team at the ETH Zurich had a key role in the development of Event-B and the Rodin project. Thank you very much!

We would also like to thank Cliff Jones, who never gave up the quest to improve the Rodin documentation, and Ken Robinson, who contributed the Event-B Cheat Sheet[3].

We are grateful to the editorial team that made this book possible in the first place, consisting of Daniel Plagge, Lukas Ladenberger and Joy Clark. We also thank Prof. Michael Leuschel, department head of the institute of software

---

[2]http://www.systerel.fr

[3]The URL of the resource is: http://handbook.event-b.org/current/files/EventB-Summary.pdf

technology and programming languages at the University of Düsseldorf, who supported us in pursuing this project.

The icons that you find throughout this handbook were created by Pixel-Mixer[4], who provides them for free. Thanks!

The cover picture was taken by Miikka Skaffari, who made it available via the Creative Commons by-nc license, depicting a sculpture by Rodin. Thanks!

1.5 DEPLOY

This work has been sponsored by the DEPLOY project[5]. DEPLOY is a European Commission Information and Communication Technologies FP7 project.

The overall aim of the EC Information and Communication Technologies FP7 DEPLOY Project is to make major advances in engineering methods for dependable systems through the deployment of formal engineering methods. Formal engineering methods enable greater mastery of complexity than found in traditional software engineering processes. It is the central role played by mechanically-analysed formal models throughout the system development flow that enables mastery of complexity.

As well as leading to big improvements in system dependability, greater mastery of complexity also leads to greater productivity by reducing the expensive test-debug-rework cycle and by facilitating increased reuse of software.

The goal of the project is to achieve and evaluate industrial take-up of DEPLOY's methods and tools (which started with DEPLOY's industrial partners) as well as to perform further research on methods and tools that is considered necessary.

1.6 Creative Commons Legal Code

---

[4]http://pixel-mixer.com/
[5]http://www.deploy-project.eu/

Chapter 2

Tutorial

The objective of this tutorial is to get you to a stage where you can use Rodin and build Event-B models. We expect you to have a basic understanding of logic and an idea why doing formal modelling is a good idea. You should be able to work through the tutorial with little or no outside help.

This tutorial covers installation and configuration for Rodin. It will teach you step by step how to build formal models. It also provides the essential theory and provides links to further information.

We attempt to alternate between theory and practical application and thereby keep you motivated. We encourage you not to download solutions to the examples but instead to actively build them up yourself as the tutorial progresses.

If something is unclear, remember to check the Reference chapter (Chapter 3) for more information.

2.1 Outline

Background before getting started (2.2) We give a brief description of what Event-B is, what it is being used for and what kind of background knowledge we expect.

Installation (2.3) We guide you through downloading, installing and starting Rodin and point out platform differences. We install the provers. We list the different window views and describe what they do.

The First Machine (2.4) We introduce our first example: a traffic light machine that uses boolean values for signals. We introduce guards, which allow the proof obligations to be automatically discharged. We explain how proof labels are read without changing to the proof perspective.

Mathematical notation (2.5) At this point we quickly go through the most important aspects of predicate calculus and provide links to the reference chapter and to external literature. We explain everything used by the traffic light system, we introduce all data types and we provide a brief intoduction of sets and relations. We also explain the difference between predicates and expressions. For example, this is where we explain the difference between TRUE and ⊤.

Introducing Contexts (2.6) We introduce contexts to apply the theoretical concepts that were introduced in the previous section. We use the Agatha-Puzzle as an example to step by step introduce more and more complex elements. We cover theorems and also mention well-definedness.

Event-B Concepts (2.7) This is another theoretical section that provides more background information about the previous examples. We analyze the anatomy of a machine and introduce all the elements that a machine or context may have. We describe the sees and refines concepts which will be applied in the next section, and we briefly mention concepts like data refinement and witnesses although we do not explain them in detail.

Expanding the Traffic Light System (2.8) We apply what we learned in the previous section by introducing a context with traffic light colors and a refinement to integrate them. We will introduce another refinement to model the push buttons.

Proving (2.9) So far all proof obligations have been discharged automatically. Now we switch to the proving perspective and explore it for the first time. We edit the configuration for the auto prover, invalidate proofs and show that with the new configuration they will not be discharged any more. We carry out a simple proof manually and describe the provers available.

Proving Deadlock Freeness (2.10) In this section we define what it means for a machine to be deadlock free. We use a more complex example to explore how much the Rodin provers can accomplish.

Outlook (2.11) This concludes the tutorial. We provide many links here for further reading. In particular, we reference the documentation from the Deploy project and the Rodin Wiki.

2.2   Before Getting Started

Before we get started with the actual tutorial, we are going to go over the required background information to make sure that you have a rudimentary understanding of the necessary concepts.

✓   **You can skip this section, if...**

- ... you know what formal modelling is
- ... you know what predicate logic is
- ... you know what Event-B and Rodin are
- ... you know what Eclipse is

2.2.1 Systems Development

Ultimately, the purpose of the methods and tools introduced here is to improve systems development. By this we mean the design and management of complex engineering projects over their life cycle. Examples include cars, air traffic control systems, etc.

"Taking an interdisciplinary approach to engineering systems is inherently complex since the behaviour of and interaction among system components is not always immediately well defined or understood. Defining and characterizing such systems and subsystems and the interactions among them is one of the goals of systems engineering. In doing so, the gap that exists between informal requirements from users, operators, marketing organisations, and technical specifications is successfully bridged."[1]

2.2.2 Formal Modelling

We are concerned with *formalizing specifications*. Formal models allow us to perform a more rigorous analysis of our system (thereby improving the quality) and allow us to reuse the specification in the development an implementation. This comes at the cost of higher up-front investments.

This differs from the traditional development process. In a formal development, we transfer some effort from the test phase (where the implementation is verified) to the specification phase (where the specification in relation to the requirements is verified).

2.2.3 Predicate Logic

In predicate logic, statements (which are called predicates) can be expressed with variables that can be quantified (e.g. "for all values of x ..."). Event-B uses predicate logic with the following features:

- Predicates and expressions are distinguished.

- All expressions have a data type, e.g. integer or set of integers.

- Quantification over variables, not predicates, is supported. This includes quantification over sets.

- A partial function semantics is included, e.g. the predicate $1 \div 0 = 1 \div 0$ is not a tautology because $1 \div 0$ does not represent a valid value.

- Comprehension sets are supported.

- Predicates can be evaluated to a Boolean value.

---

[1]http://en.wikipedia.org/wiki/Systems_engineering#Managing_complexity

2.2.4   Event-B

Event-B is a notation for formal modelling based around an abstract machine notation.

Event-B is considered an evolution of B (also known as classical B). It is a simpler notation which is easier to learn and use. It comes with tool support in the form of the Rodin Platform.

2.2.5   Rodin

Rodin (3.1) is the name of the tool platform for Event-B. It allows formal Event-B models to be created with an editor. It generates proof obligations (3.2.7) that can be discharged either automatically or interactively.

Rodin is a modular software and many extensions are available. These include alternative editors, document generators, team support, and extensions (called plugins) some of which include support decomposition and records. An up-to-date list of plugins is maintained in the Rodin Wiki (1.1.2)[2].

2.2.6   Eclipse

Rodin is based on the Eclipse Platform (3.1.1), a Java-based platform for building software tools. This is important for two reasons:

- If you have already used Eclipse-based software, then you will feel immediately comfortable with how Rodin applications are handled.

- Many extensions, or plugins, are available for Eclipse-based software. There are Rodin-specific plugins as well as plugins independent of Rodin that may be useful to you. The Rodin Wiki (1.1.2), contains a list of plugins is maintained.

The GUI of an Eclipse application consists of views, editors, toolbars, quickviews, perspectives and many more elements. If these terms are unfamiliar to you, please consult Section 3.1.1 which contains references to Eclipse tutorials.

In Section 2.3, we present the Rodin-specific GUI elements.

2.3   Installation

 Goals: The objective of this section is to guide you through downloading, installing and starting Rodin. In addition, we explain the update mechanisms needed to install new plugins for Rodin. Finally, we name the Rodin-specific GUI elements and describe their functions.

You can skip this section, if. . .

---

[2]These links were valid at the time of the writing of this document:
http://wiki.event-b.org/index.php/Rodin_plugins
http://wiki.event-b.org/index.php/Installing_external_plugins_manually

- ... you know how to install and update Rodin
- ... you know how to install new plugins for Rodin

 Rodin is fairly resource intensive. You need a good computer with plenty of memory to run it. It is recommended to have at least 2GB of RAM.

2.3.1 Install Rodin for the first time

Step 1: Download

The first step is to download Rodin. Rodin is available for download on the Rodin Download page. There is also a link for the download site in the faq (4.1.6).

Rodin is available for Windows, Mac OS, and Linux. For all the platforms, the distribution is always available for download as a zip file. Download the zip file for your system anywhere on your PC.

 It is recommended that you download the latest stable version.

Step 2: Install and Run Rodin

 Rodin is easy to install on the platforms for which a prebuild version exists. If no prebuild version exists for your platform, please check out Section 4.1.8 in the FAQ on suggestions for how to install Rodin

To install Rodin, extract the contents of the zip file to a desired directory. You can run the tool by using the `rodin` executable.

Starting Rodin should bring up a welcome screen. It provides some quick guidance for Rodin. In particular, it provides instructions on installing the provers.

 Please install the provers right away. It is easy and only takes a few clicks.

After dismissing the welcome screen, you should see the window shown in Figure 2.1. Here you can specify the path where Rodin stores your projects.

After specifying a path click the OK button. Rodin will start and the window shown in Figure 2.2 will open.

 When using a Linux distribution, a welcome window may open up. Exit out of this window to get to the main screen. Other problems can also occur when installing Rodin in Linux. See the release notes for details.[3]

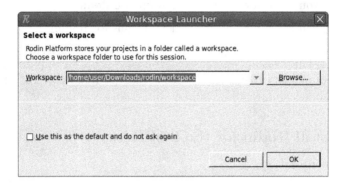

Figure 2.1: Eclipse Workspace Launcher

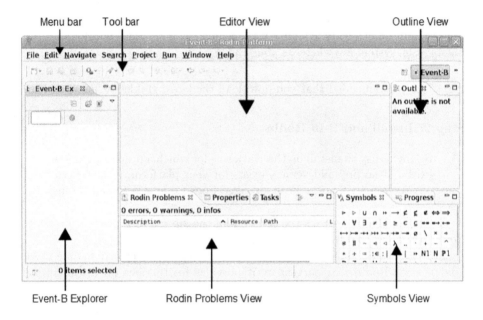

Figure 2.2: Rodin GUI

As already mentioned in Section 2.2.6, the GUI of an Eclipse application consists of views, editors, toolbars, quickviews, perspectives and many more elements. Here we list the different Rodin GUI elements (i.e. views) which are visible after starting Rodin for the first time and explain their functions:

Menu bar (3.1.2) The menu bar of the Rodin programs provides file and edit operations as well as other commands.

Tool bar (3.1.2) The tool bar provides short cuts for commonly used com-

---
[3] See Rodin Release Notes

mands such as save, print, undo and redo.

Event-B Explorer (3.1.2) The Event-B Explorer shows the projects' tree structure. Projects are the main entries in this view, and when a project is expanded, the corresponding project files will also be shown.

Outline View (3.1.2) The Outline view shows the outline of the active editor or file.

Rodin Problems View (3.1.2) The Rodin Problems view displays problems (e.g., syntax errors) from the currently active projects.

Symbols View (3.1.2) The Symbols view shows a list of available mathematical symbols which can be used in conjunction with the mathematical notation (3.3).

Editor View (3.1.2) The Editor view displays the active editor and is the view in which Event-B files are edited.

2.3.2 Install new plugins

This sections describes how to install new plugins for Rodin by using the example of the Atelier B Provers plugin (3.4.4). It is highly recommended that you install this plugin because it will not be possible to prove much without it.

Open the Install Manager Help ⟩ Install New Software.... Click the downward arrow next to the field Work with to select the Atelier B Provers update site. Check the box next to the Atelier B Provers entry and click on the Next button (compare with Figure 2.3). Follow the installation instruction to install the plugin. After installing the plugin, you will be asked to restart Rodin in order to finalize the installation.

 If you are using a firewall, you may need to change the proxy settings.

2.4 The First Machine: A Traffic Light Controller

 Goals: The objective of this section is to get acquainted with the modelling environment. We will create a very simple model consisting of just one file to develop a feeling for Rodin and Event-B.

In this tutorial, we will create a model of a traffic light controller. We will use this example repeatedly in subsequent sections. Figure 2.4 depicts what we are trying to achieve.

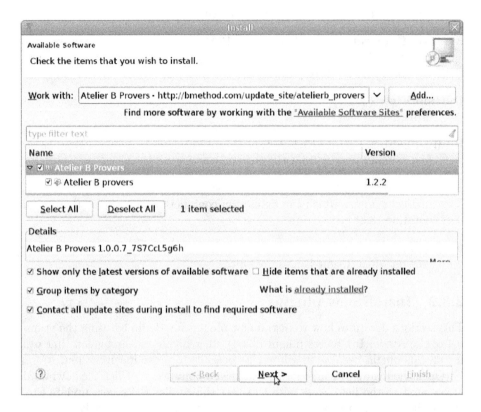

Figure 2.3: Eclipse Install Manager

There is a four-page Event-B Cheat Sheet[4], representing a concise summary of the Event-B mathematical toolkit. Thanks to Ken Robinson for making it available.

In this section, we will implement a simplified controller with the following characteristics:

- We will model the signals with Boolean values to indicate "stop" (false) and "go" (true). We do not model colors (yet) because we think we should first specify our goal (regulating the traffic) and later add implementation details (the traffic light's colors).

- To keep the initial model simple, we will not include the push button yet. We will add it later.

---

[4]The URL of the resource is: http://handbook.event-b.org/current/files/EventB-Summary.pdf

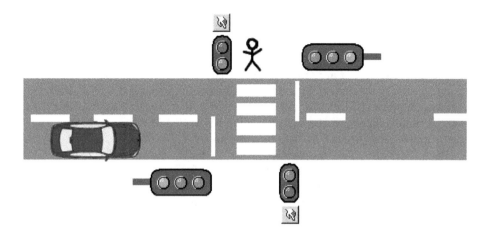

Figure 2.4: The traffic light controller

2.4.1 Excursus: The specification process

While this handbook is concerned with use of the Rodin tool, it is important to understand the specification process as well. It can be daunting and unclear especially for beginners to recognize where to start with the model, what kind of data structures and abstractions to use, and so on.

We cover a few examples in this chapter that should develop your ability to answer these questions implicitly, but there is no explicit set of instructions. For example, we will first model the traffic lights as Boolean values and later refine them into actual colors. But how did we come up with this refinement strategy? Likewise, we decided to add the push buttons at a later refinement. In retrospect this may seem useful, but it is still not clear how we arrived at this structure in the first place.

Jean-Raymond Abrial has something to say about this in his book[5]. Some of the chapters are available in the Rodin Wiki.

ЧR   It takes some time to learn how to read formal specifications, and not all stakeholders are willing to learn it. Further, textual re-quiremenets are almost always the starting point for a formal specification. It would be nice to kep a traceability to the origianl requirements.

ProR is a tool for editing requirements. An integration with Rodin exists, which allows a traceability between textual requirements and model elements to be established. This shows the Event-B model elements seamless as part of

---

[5]http://www.amazon.com/Modeling-Event-B-System-Software-Engineering/dp/0521895561

the textual requirements. The various traceability options are demonstrated in the Formal Mind Blog.

Further, the traces are tracked, and if the source or the target of a trace changes, a marker is set, so that the changes can be inspected and verified.

Being able to set traces is not enough, if there is not a theory behind it to make it useful. One such theory is based on the WRSPM reference model. How this works in practice can be seen in this paper.

Last, ProR is based on the ReqIF standard, which is supported by major industry tools for requirements management (like Rational DOORS or PTC integrity). This eases the integration of Event-B into existing development processes.

This contribution requires the **ProR Requirements** plugin. The content is maintained by the plugin contributors and may be out of date.

2.4.2   Project Setup

Models typically consist of multiple files that are managed in a project. Create a new Event-B Project File ⟩ New ⟩ Event-B Project. Give the project the name `tutorial-03` as shown in Figure 2.5.

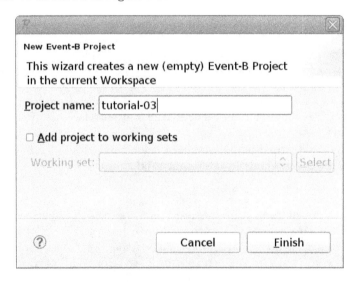

Figure 2.5: New Event-B Project Wizard

 Eclipse supports different types of projects. The project must have the Rodin Nature (3.1.1) to work. A project can have more than one nature.

Next, create a new Event-B Component. Either use File ⟩ New ⟩ Event-B Component or right-click on the newly created project and select New ⟩ Event-B Component. Use `mac` as the component name, select Machine as component-type, and click Finish as shown in Figure 2.6. This will create a Machine (3.2.4) file.

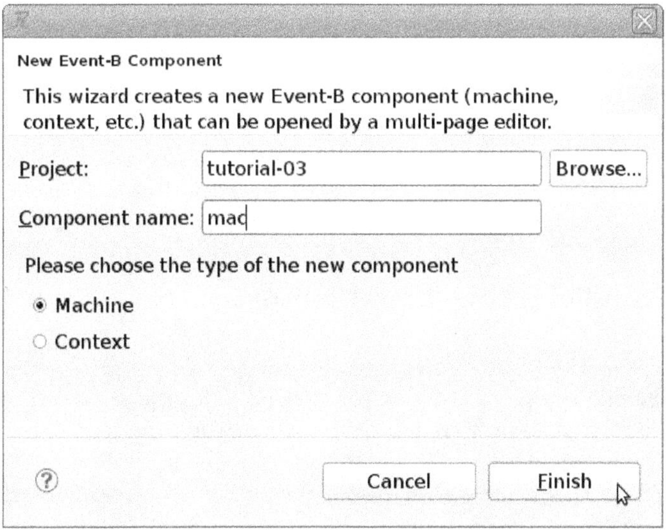

Figure 2.6: New Event-B Component Wizard

The newly created component will open in the Rodin Editor. This displays the machine hierarchy as text, although at this point, you cannot add any text apart from comments. Elements can be added to the model by using the wizards for variables, variants, invariants, and events (the ∨, ∨, ι, and ℯ buttons).

You can also add elements by finding the name of the machine under the MACHINE heading. There is a small green arrow (⟩) directly to the right of the name of the machine (in this case, the name of the machine is "mac"). Place your cursor directly to the left of the green arrow and right click. Select the element that you would like to add from the Add Child menu. If an element of a certain type has already been created, you can also create more elements of that type by right clicking on the type of the element you would like to add (e.g. VARIABLES) that is coloured in purple and select Add Child. You can also place your cursor directly before the green arrow to the left of an element name and hit CTRL-T or right click and select Add Sibling.

You can also edit the machine using the Event-B Machine Editor. This was the default editor in Rodin 2.3 and earlier versions and is still available to view and edit machine files. To do this, right click on the `mac` component in the Event-B Explorer and select Open With ⟩ Event-B Machine Editor. This editor has four tabs at the bottom. The Pretty Print tab shows the model as a whole with color highlighting, but it cannot be edited here. This is useful to inspect the model. Under the Edit tab, you can edit the model. The six main sections of a machine (REFINES, SEES, etc.) are displayed in a collapsed state. You can click on the ▷ button to the left of a section to expand it.

This editor is *form-based*. This means that it can be modified by using controls (i.e. text fields, dropdowns, etc.) to input information. More information about this editor is available in the reference section (3.1.5).

 Alternative editors are available as plugins. The form editor has the advantage of guiding the user through the model, but it takes up a lot of space and can be slow for big models. The text-based Camille Editor (2.4.3) is very popular. Please visit the Rodin Wiki (1.1.2) for the latest information.

2.4.3   Camille, a text-based editor

 Camille is a "real" text editor that provides the same feel as a typical Eclipse text editor and provides all of the functions that most text editors provide (i.e. copy, paste, undo, redo, etc.) However, please note that at this time not all Rodin plugins are compatible with Camille. For more information, please consult the extensive documentation in the Rodin Wiki (1.1.2).

Camille can be installed via its update site, which is preconfigured in Rodin. Once installed, Camille will be set as the default editor. The rodin editor or structural editor can still be used by selecting it from the context menu of a file in the project browser.

For more information, please visit `http://wiki.event-b.org/index.php/Text_Editor`.

This contribution requires the **Camille** plugin. The content is maintained by the plugin contributors and may be out of date.

2.4.4   Building the Model

Back to the problem: Our objective is to build a simplified traffic light controller as described in 2.4. We start with the model state. Two traffic lights will be modelled, and we will therefore create two variables called `cars_go` and `peds_go`.

Creating Variables

Under the MACHINE heading, you see the machine name mac. There is a small green arrow (⚘) to the right of this label. Place your cursor directly to the left of the green arrow, right click, and select Add Child ⟩ Event-B Variable to add a new variable. Optionally, you can also use the New Variable Wizard (the button ⚘) to create your variable.

By default, the variable is named var1. Place your cursor inside the var1 label. The label will then turn into a textbox. Change the name to cars_go. You can add a comment to the variable by placing your cursor to the right of the little green arrow and typing into the text box that appears.

 Comments: The comment field does not support line breaks, nor is is possible to "comment out" parts of the model as it is with most programming languages.

Create the second variable (peds_go) in the same way, or place your cursor directly to the left of the small green arrow next to the label cars_go and hit either CTRL-T or right click and select Add Sibling from the menu.

Upon saving, the variables will be underlined in red which indicates that an error is present as shown in Figure 2.7. The Rodin Problems view (3.1.2) shows corresponding error messages. In this case, the error message is "Variable cars_go does not have a type".

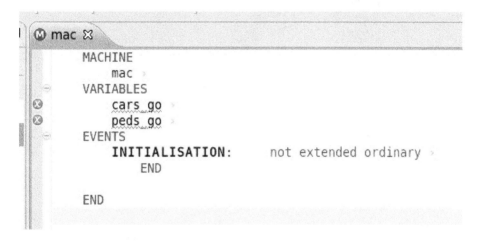

Figure 2.7: Red highlighted elements indicate errors

Invariants are needed in order to specify the type of variables. Use the method described above to add invariants to your machine (except this time select Add Child ⟩ Event-B Invariant from the menu or click the ᶦᵗ button to open up the New Invariant Wizard). Add two invariants (which will automatically be labelled inv1 and inv2). The actual invariant appears to the left of the label and is prepopulated with the symbol ⊤, which represents the logical value "true". Placing your cursor inside the invariant field will change it to a text field and allow editing.

Change the first invariant (the symbol ⊤, not the label inv1) to $cars\_go \in BOOL$ and the second invariant to $peds\_go \in BOOL$. Event-B provides the build-in datatype BOOL among others (3.3.1).

Mathematical Symbols: Every mathematical symbol has an ASCII-representation and the substitution occurs automatically. To generate "element of" ($\in$), simply type a colon ("`:`"). The editor will perform the substitution after a short delay. The Symbols view shows all supported mathematical symbols. The ASCII representation of a symbol can be found by hovering over the symbol in question. Symbols can also be added manually by selecting them from the Symbols view

After saving, you should see that the INITIALISATION event is underlined in yellow with a small warning sign to the left as demonstrated in Figure 2.8. Again, the Rodin Problems view displays the error message: "Variable cars_go is not initialized". Every variable must be initialized in a way that is consistent with the model.

```
VARIABLES
      cars_go  ›
      peds_go  ›
INVARIANTS
      inv2:    peds_go ∈ BOOL      not theorem      ›
      inv1:    cars_go ∈ BOOL      not theorem      ›
EVENTS
      INITIALISATION:          not extended ordinary  ›
            END

END
```

Figure 2.8: Yellow highlighted elements indicate warnings

To fix this problem, place your cursor to the left of the small green arrow next to the label INITIALISATION. Right click and add an Event-B Action. Repeat to add another event. In the action fields, enter $cars\_go := FALSE$ and $peds\_go := FALSE$.

State Transitions with Events

Our traffic light controller cannot yet change its state. To make this possible, we create two events (3.2.4) in the manner described above and name them set_peds_go and set_peds_stop. This will model the traffic light for the pedestrians, and for each of these, we will add an Event-B action to each of the events. These actions will change peds_go to TRUE or FALSE, which simulates the changing of the traffic light.

 From now on, we won't describe the individual steps in the editor any more. Instead, we will simply show the resulting model.

The two events will look as follows:

Event   *set_peds_go* $\widehat{=}$
    begin
        act1 : *peds_go* := *TRUE*
    end
Event   *set_peds_stop* $\widehat{=}$
    begin
        act1 : *peds_go* := *FALSE*
    end

Event parameters

For the traffic light for the cars, we present a different approach and use only one event with a parameter. The event will use the new traffic light state as the argument. For this, we need to add an Event-B Event Parameter, which will appear under the heading ANY, and an Event-B Guard, which will appear under the heading WHERE:

Event   *set_cars* $\widehat{=}$
    any
        new_value
    where
        grd1 : *new_value* $\in$ *BOOL*
    then
        act1 : *cars_go* := *new_value*
    end

Note how the parameter is used in the action block to set the new state.

Invariants

If this model was actually in control of a traffic light, we would have a problem because nothing is preventing the model from setting both traffic lights to TRUE. The reason is that so far we only modeled the domain (the traffic lights and their states) and not the requirements. We have the following safety requirement:

REQ-1: Both traffic lights must not be TRUE at the same time.

We can model this requirement with the following invariant:

$$\neg(cars\_go = TRUE \wedge peds\_go = TRUE)$$

Please add this invariant with the label `inv3` to the model (Use the ASCII codes **not** and **&** to get the symbols $\neg$ and $\wedge$).

Obviously, this invariant can be violated, and Rodin informs us of this. The Event-B Explorer (3.1.2) provides this information in various ways. Go to the

explorer and expand the project (`tutorial-03`), the machine (`mac`) and the
entry "Proof Obligations". You should see four proof obligations, two of which
are discharged (marked with) and two of which are not discharged (marked
with).

Proof obligations: A proof obligation is something that has to be
proven to show the consistency of the machine, the correctness of
theorems, etc. A proof obligation consists of a label, a number of
hypothesis that can be used in the proof and a goal – a predicate that
must be proven. Have a look at the proof obligation labels. They
indicate the origin in the model where they were generated. E.g.
set_peds_go/inv3/INV is the proof obligation that must be verified
to show that the event set_peds_go preserves the invariant (INV)
with the label inv3. An overview about all labels can be found
in Section 3.2.7. The proof obligations can also be found via other
entries in the explorer, like the events they belong to. Elements that
have non-discharged proof obligations as children are marked with
a small question mark. For instance, `inv3` has all proof obligations
as children, while the event `set_cars` has one.

To prevent the invariant from being violated (and therefore to allow all proof
obligations to be discharged), we need to strengthen the guards (3.2.4) of the
events.

 Before looking at the solution, try to fix the model yourself.

Finding Invariant Violations with ProB

 A useful tool for understanding and debugging a model is a model
checker like ProB. You can install ProB directly from Rodin by using
the ProB Update Site. Just select Install New Software... from the Help
menu and select "ProB" from the dropdown. You should see "ProB for
Rodin2" as an installation option, which you can then install using the normal
Eclipse mechanism.

We will continue the example at the point where we added the safety invariant (REQ-1), but didn't add guards yet to prevent the invariants from being
violated.

We launch ProB by right-clicking on the machine we'd like to animate
and select Start Animation / Model Checking. Rodin will switch to the ProB-
Perspective, as shown in Figure 2.9. The top left pane shows the available events
of the machines. Upon starting, only INITIALISATION is enabled. The middle
pane shows the current state of the machine, and the right pane shows a history. On the bottom of the main pane we can see whether any errors occurred,
like invariant violations. We can now interact with the model by triggering

events. This is done by double-clicking on an enabled event or by right-clicking it and selecting a set of parameters, if applicable. We first trigger INITIAL-ISATION. After that, all events are enabled. Next, we trigger set_cars and set_peds_go with the parameter *TRUE*. As expected, we will get an invariant violation. In the state view, we can "drill down" and find out which invariant was violated, and the history view shows us how we reached this state (Figure 2.10). After modifying a machine, ProB has to be restarted, which is done again by right-clicking the machine and selecting ProB. Triggering events to find invariant violations is not very efficient. But ProB can perform model checking automatically. To do so, select Model Checking from the Checks menu from the "Events" View (the view on the left). After optionally adjusting some parameters, the model checking can be triggered by pressing "Start Consistency Checking". Upon completion, the result of the check is shown. ProB has many more functions and also supports additional formalisms. Please visit the ProB Website for more information.

This contribution requires the **ProB** plugin. The content is maintained by the plugin contributors and may be out of date.

2.4.5 The Final Traffic Light Model

MACHINE mac
VARIABLES
    cars_go
    peds_go
INVARIANTS
    inv1 : $cars\_go \in BOOL$
    inv2 : $peds\_go \in BOOL$
    inv3 : $\neg(cars\_go = TRUE \wedge peds\_go = TRUE)$
EVENTS
Initialisation
    begin
        act1 : $cars\_go := FALSE$
        act2 : $peds\_go := FALSE$
    end
Event *set_peds_go* $\widehat{=}$
    when
        grd1 : $cars\_go = FALSE$
    then
        act1 : $peds\_go := TRUE$
    end
Event *set_peds_stop* $\widehat{=}$
    begin
        act1 : $peds\_go := FALSE$

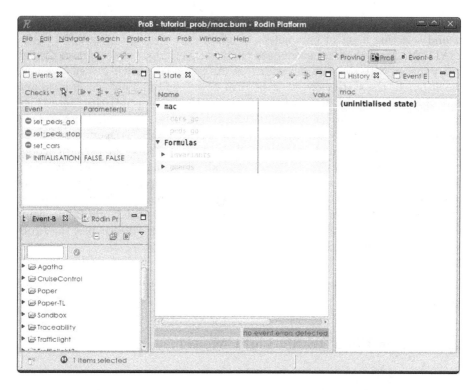

Figure 2.9: The ProB Perspective

```
        end
Event   set_cars ≙
     any
          new_value
     where
          grd1 :  new_value ∈ BOOL
          grd2 :  new_value = TRUE ⇒ peds_go = FALSE
     then
          act1 :  cars_go := new_value
     end
END
```

2.5   Mathematical notation

✓ **Goals:** In order to understand how basic properties of a model can
be expressed in Event-B, we need a brief introduction of predicates,
terms and data types.

In Event-B, we use a mathematical notation to describe the systems we want
to model. This allows us to be very precise about the model's properties.

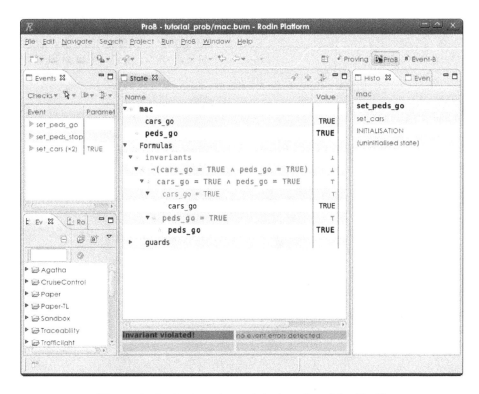

Figure 2.10: An invariant violation, found by ProB

2.5.1 Predicates

In the traffic light example, we have already encountered several predicates: The invariants of a model and the guards of an event. The proof obligations generated by Rodin are also predicates. A predicate is simply an expression, the value of which is either true or false.

The simplest predicates are ⊤ (ASCII: `true`) and ⊥ (ASCII: `false`). We can also assert if arbitrary objects of the same type are equal with = or not equal with ≠ (ASCII: `/=`). Predicates can be combined with the usual logical operators:

	symbol	ASCII
conjunction (and)	∧	`&`
disjunction (or)	∨	`or`
implication	⇒	`=>`
equivalence	⇔	`<=>`
negation (not)	¬	`not`

We can use *universal quantification* to express a statement that is valid for all possible values a variable might have. The universal quantifier is ∀ (ASCII: `!`).

For example, in order to show that any given number x greater than zero and multiplied with two is greater than one, we can use the following expression:

$$\forall x \cdot x > 0 \Rightarrow 2 \cdot x > 1 \qquad \text{ASCII: !x. x>0 => 2*x > 1}$$

When a variable is introduced by a quantifier, the type of the variable must be clear. In this case Rodin can infer that x must be of type integer because the operator $<$ is defined only on integers. Sometimes the type cannot be inferred, e.g., in

$$\forall a, b \cdot a \neq b \Rightarrow b \neq a \qquad \text{ASCII: !a,b. a/=b => b/=a}$$

a and b could be integers, Boolean values or some other type. In this case, we must make the type of the variables explicit by stating that a and b are elements of the appropriate sets. Let's use integers again to correct the previous expression:

$$\forall a, b \cdot a \in \mathbb{Z} \wedge b \in \mathbb{Z} \wedge a \neq b \Rightarrow b \neq a$$

$$\text{ASCII: !a,b. a:INT \& b:INT \& a/=b => b/=a}$$

The conjunction operator ($\wedge$) has a stronger binding that the implication $\Rightarrow$, so the above expression is equivalent to

$$\forall a, b \cdot (a \in \mathbb{Z} \wedge b \in \mathbb{Z} \wedge a \neq b) \Rightarrow b \neq a$$

> ⚠ If you are unsure which of the operators bind stronger, we advise you to use parenthesis to avoid mistakes.

Existential quantification on the other hand is used to state that there is an object of a certain type fulfilling a given property. The existential quantifier is $\exists$ (ASCII: #). The following example expression states that there is a Boolean value different from TRUE:

$$\exists x \cdot x \in \text{BOOL} \wedge x \neq \text{TRUE} \qquad \text{ASCII: \#x. x:BOOL \& x/=TRUE}$$

As you can see, we again added type information for x. We put the type information on the left side of the implication ($\Rightarrow$) for the universal quantification , but for existential quantification we add it via a conjunction ($\wedge$).

2.5.2   Data types

We have seen that each identifier (i.e. a variable, constant or parameter) must have a distinguished type. If we can introduce an identifier anywhere, we usually must also add a predicate with which the identifier's type can be determined. In the traffic light example, a variable **cars_go** was introduced and the type was set by an invariant $cars\_go \in \text{BOOL}$. In the next section, we'll see that the type of constants is set by axioms (also predicates) and later we'll see that the type for parameters will be determined by using guards (again, predicates).

As a rule, each term in Event-B must have a certain type. When saving a Event-B component, Rodin starts the type checker to ensure that types are correctly used. For example, the terms on both sides of an equality (=) must have the same type. If this is not the case, Rodin will generate an error message. For each type there exists a set that denotes exactly all elements that belong the type. We will now briefly give an overview about all types you might encounter.

Integers We have already seen numbers, which are of type integer ($\mathbb{Z}$). Example terms of type $\mathbb{Z}$ are 5, $x + 7$ and $7 \cdot y - 3$.

Booleans We have already seen the Boolean type (BOOL) in the previous section (2.4). It has exactly two elements, BOOL = {TRUE, FALSE}.

Carrier sets A user can introduce a new type by adding its name to the Sets section of a context. We see that in more detail in the next section (2.6).

Sets If we have terms of a certain type, we can easily construct sets of that type. E.g. 1 and $2 \cdot x$ denote integers ($\mathbb{Z}$) and $\{1, 2 \cdot x\}$ is a set of integers ($\mathbb{P}(\mathbb{Z})$). $\mathbb{P}(S)$ (ASCII: POW) denotes the power set (the set of all subsets) of S.

Pairs If we have two terms, we can construct a pair. For example, with 2 and TRUE, we can construct the pair $2 \mapsto$ TRUE (ASCII: 2|->TRUE). The type of that pair is $\mathbb{Z} \times$ BOOL, where $\times$ denotes the Cartesian product. Set of pairs ("relations") play an important role in modelling languages like Event-B.

 Please do not confuse predicates and Boolean values! For example, if you want to express the condition "if the variable b is true, x should be greater than 2", you *cannot* write $b \Rightarrow x > 2$ (That would produce a syntax error). Instead you have to write $b =$ TRUE $\Rightarrow x > 2$.

In Section 3.3 the types of each operator in Event-B are described in detail.

2.5.3 Operations on Sets

Let's assume that we have two sets A and B of the same type, e.g. sets of integers. Then we can check if an element e is in it with the expression $e \in A$ (ASCII: e:A) or on if it is not in A with $e \notin A$ (ASCII: e/:A). Expressing that all elements of A are also elements of B (i.e. A is a subset of B) can be done with the expression $A \subseteq B$ (ASCII: A<:B). The negated form is $A \not\subseteq B$ (ASCII: A/<:B).

We can build the union $A \cup B$, the intersection $A \cap B$ and the set subtraction $A \setminus B$ (ASCII: A\/B, A/\B and A\B). The set subtraction contains all elements that are in A but not in B.

The power set $\mathbb{P}(A)$ (ASCII: POW(A)) is the set of all subsets of A. Thus $B \in \mathbb{P}(A)$ is equivalent to $B \subseteq A$. $\mathbb{P}_1(A)$ (ASCII: POW1(A)) is the set of all non-empty subsets of A.

2.5.4   Introducing user-defined types

We can introduce our own new types simply by giving such types a name. This is done by adding the name of the type to the *SETS* section of a context. We will see how this is done in practice in the next section (2.6).

For instance, if we want to model different kind of fruits in our model, we might create the set $FRUITS$. Then the identifier $FRUITS$ denotes the set of all elements of this type. Nothing more is known about $FRUITS$ unless we add further axioms. In particular, we do not know the cardinality (number of elements) of the set or even if it is finite.

 Assume that we want to model *apples* and *oranges* which are sub-sets of $FRUITS$. We do not need to introduce them in the *SETS* section of a context just because they are sets. Let's imagine such a scenario where *apples* and *oranges* are modelled as types of their own (by declaring them in the *SETS* section). And we have two variables or constants a and o with $a \in apples$ and $o \in oranges$. Then we cannot compare a and o with $a = o$ or $a \neq o$. That would raise a type error because $=$ and $\neq$ expect the same type for the left and right expression.

If we want to model sub-sets *apples* and *oranges* as described above, we can add them as constants and state that $apples \subseteq FRUITS$ and $oranges \subseteq FRUITS$. If apples and oranges are all fruits we want to model, we can assume $apples \cup oranges = FRUITS$ and if no fruit is both an apple and orange we can write $apples \cap oranges = \varnothing$. A shorter way to express this is to say that apples and oranges constitute a partition of the fruits: $partition(FRUITS, apples, oranges)$. In general, we can use the partition operator to express that a set S is partitioned by the sets $s_1, \ldots, s_n$ with $partition(S, s_1, \ldots, s_n)$. We use partitions in Section 2.6.2.

Another typical usage for user defined data types are *enumerated sets*. These are sets where we know all the elements already. Let's take a system which can be either working or broken. We model this by introducing a type $STATUS$ in the *SETS* section and two constants *working* and *broken*. We define that STATUS consists of exactly *working* and *broken* by $STATUS = \{working, broken\}$. Additionally, we have to say that *working* and *broken* are not the same by $working \neq broken$.

If the enumerated sets gets larger, we need to state for every two element of the set that they are distinct. Thus, for a set of 10 constants, we'll need $(10^2 - 10) \div 2 = 45$ predicates. Again, we can use the partition operator to express this in a more concise way:

$$partition(STATUS, \{working\}, \{broken\})$$

2.5.5   Relations

Relations are a powerful instrument when modelling systems. From a mathematical point of view, a relation is just a set of pairs. Formally, when we have two sets A and B, we can specify that r is a relation between both by $r \in \mathbb{P}(A \times B)$ (ASCII: `r:POW(A**B)`). Because relations are so common, there is also a symbol to denote a relation, so a shorter way to write the above expression is $r \in A \leftrightarrow B$ (ASCII: `r:A<->B`).

With $a \mapsto b \in r$, we can check if two elements a and b are related in respect to b.

We use a small example to illustrate relations. Let $A = \{a, b, c, d\}$ and $B = \{1, 2, 3, 4\}$. We define the relation r with $r = \{a \mapsto 1, a \mapsto 3, c \mapsto 2, d \mapsto 1\}$. The *domain* of r are all elements occurring on the left side $\mathrm{dom}(r) = \{a, c, d\}$ and the *range* are all elements on the right $\mathrm{ran}(r) = \{1, 2, 3\}$.

To find out to which elements the objects of the set $s = \{b, c, d\}$ are related to, we can use the *relational image*: $r[s] = r[\{b, c, d\}] = \{1, 2\}$. Often we want to know to which object a single element a is related. We just write it as a singleton set: $r[\{a\}] = \{1, 3\}$.

Event-B supports several operators to work with relations (3.3.5). We will not go into more detail during the course of the tutorial.

An important special case of relations are functions. Functions are relations where each element of the domain is uniquely related to one element of the range. Event-B directly supports operators to describe partial and total functions, which can be injective, surjective or bijective.

2.5.6 Arithmetic

We have the usual operations on integers, $+$, $-$, $\cdot$ and $\div$ (ASCII: `+`, `-`, `*` and `/`). They can be compared with the usual equality operators: $<, \leq, \geq, >$ (ASCII: `<, <=, >=, >`).

$\mathbb{Z}$ (ASCII: `INT`) denotes the set of all integer numbers. $\mathbb{N}$ and $\mathbb{N}_1$ (ASCII: `NAT` and `NAT1` respectively) are the subsets of natural numbers.

 If you specify two variables x and y with $x \in \mathbb{Z}$ and $y \in \mathbb{N}$, then both are of type integer ($\mathbb{Z}$). $\mathbb{N}$ is not another type. There is just the additional condition $y \geq 0$.

2.6 Introducing Contexts

 Goals: In this section we introduce contexts that apply to the theoretical concepts that were introduced in the previous section (2.5). We will create a very simple model consisting of just one context file.

In this tutorial, we will create a model of the well known Agatha puzzle. We use this instead of the already introduced traffic light example because it provides us with more possibilities to apply Event-B's logic and to use operations on relations. Here is a brief description of the puzzle:

Someone in Dreadsbury Mansion killed Aunt Agatha. Agatha, the butler, and Charles live in Dreadsbury Mansion and are the only ones to live there.

A killer always hates, and is no richer than his victim. Charles hates no one that Agatha hates. Agatha hates everybody except the butler. The butler hates everyone not richer than Aunt Agatha. The butler hates everyone whom Agatha hates. No one hates everyone. Who killed Agatha?

Contexts are used to model static properties of a model, things that do not change over time. Whereas with machines we model the dynamic properties like the traffic light above. The objective of this section is to get familiar with contexts by modelling the Agatha puzzle.

2.6.1   Create a Context

Create a new Event-B Project File 〉 New 〉 Event-B Project. Give the project the name tutorial-05.

Next, create a new Event-B Component. The process for creating a context is similar to the process for creating a machine (2.4), but this time use agatha as the component name and select the Context (3.2.3) option in order to create a Context file instead of a Machine (3.2.4) file.

Click the Finish button. Rodin should start the editor with the created Context file (see Figure 2.11).

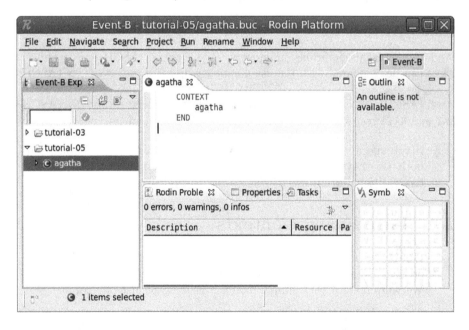

Figure 2.11: Context file opened with Rodin Editor

2.6.2   Populate the Context

In this section we model the Agatha puzzle step by step.

Modelling the Persons

We have three persons in the Agatha puzzle: Agatha herself, the butler and Charles. We model the three persons as constants (one constant for each person) in the corresponding CONSTANTS section:

CONSTANTS
 Agatha
 butler
 Charles

These constants or persons respectively are part of a set:

SETS
 persons

Now the constants themselves are not very useful since they have no type (after creating the constants, they will be highlighted in red, which indicates a problem). The semantics of the sets (3.3.4) and constants (3.2.3) are specified in the axioms (3.2.3). As already mentioned above the persons are part of the set **persons**. We model this by creating a partition (3.3.4) in the AXIOMS section:

AXIOMS
 person_partition :
  $partition(persons, \{Agatha\}, \{butler\}, \{Charles\})$

 Please note the curly braces {} around the constants. It's very easy to forget these, but if they are missing, typing errors are created which are very hard to interpret for a novice.

 The New Enumerated Set Wizard (3.1.6) allows you to create the constants, the set and the axiom automatically at the same time. To access this wizard, click on the New Enumerated Set Wizard tool bar item or find it under Event-B ⟩ New Enumerated Set Wizard. This will bring up a wizard into which we can enter the name of the set and the constants in the corresponding text fields. The wizard will create the enumerated set, the constants and the axiom automatically.

Modelling the Relations "Persons who hate each other" and "Who's how rich"

We create two more constants **hates** and **richer** to model the relations "Persons who hate each other" and "Who's how rich". The relations are abstract, which means that they say nothing about the concrete persons (Agatha, the butler and Charles). We define the concrete relationships between the persons later in this section.

The first constant **hates** is an arbitrary relation (3.3.5) between **persons**:

 AXIOMS
   hate_relation : $hates \in persons \leftrightarrow persons$

The second constant **richer** is also a relation between **persons**:

 AXIOMS
   richer_relation1 : $richer \in persons \leftrightarrow persons$

However, we know that the relation is irreflexive (no person is richer than itself):

 AXIOMS
   richer_relation2 : $richer \cap id = \varnothing$

In addition, we know that the relation is transitive:

 AXIOMS
   richer_relation3 : $(\forall x, y, z \cdot (x \mapsto y \in richer \wedge y \mapsto z \in richer) \Rightarrow x \mapsto z \in richer)$

Finally, the relation is trichotomous (one person is always richer than the other or vice versa, never both directions):

 AXIOMS
   richer_relation4 : $(\forall x, y \cdot x \in persons \wedge y \in persons \wedge x \neq y \Rightarrow (x \mapsto y \in richer \Leftrightarrow y \mapsto x \notin richer))$

Modelling the "Crime"

Since the objective of the puzzle is to find the killer, we have to create a new constant **killer** which is an element of **persons**:

 CONSTANTS
   killer
AXIOMS

killer_type : *killer* ∈ *persons*

In addition, the puzzle has some more relationships between the different persons which are all modelled as axioms. We know that the killer hates his victim and is no richer than his victim:

AXIOMS

killer_hates : *killer* ↦ *Agatha* ∈ *hates*
killer_not_richer : *killer* ↦ *Agatha* ∉ *richer*

Charles hates no one that Agatha hates and Agatha hates everybody except the butler:

AXIOMS

charles_hates : *hates*[{*Agatha*}] ∩ *hates*[{*Charles*}] = ∅
agatha_hates : *hates*[{*Agatha*}] = *persons* \ {*butler*}

The butler hates everyone not richer than aunt Agatha and the butler hates everyone whom Agatha hates. However, no one hates everyone:

AXIOMS

butler_hates_1 : ∀*x*·(*x* ↦ *Agatha* ∉ *richer* ⇒ *butler* ↦ *x* ∈ *hates*)
butler_hates_2 : *hates*[{*Agatha*}] ⊆ *hates*[{*butler*}]
noone_hates_everyone : ∀*x*·*x* ∈ *persons* ⇒ *hates*[{*x*}] ≠ *persons*

Finally, we have to model the solution:

AXIOMS

solution : *killer* = *Agatha*

All axioms are set to "not theorem" when they are created. But we need the solution to be a theorem so that we can prove that it is valid. In order to do this, click on **not theorem** shown to the right of the axiom **solution**. This box will automatically change to **theorem**, and you will have set the axiom as a theorem as shown in Figure 2.12.

```
AXIOMS
    solution:   killer = Agatha    theorem
```

Figure 2.12: Mark an Axiom as Theorem

Theorems describe properties that are expected to be able to be derived from the axioms. Therefore, to prove a theorem you only use axioms and theorems that have already been proven.

The introduced theorem still has to be proven. Thus Rodin generates a proof obligation called solution/THM. However, at this point of the tutorial we do not want to go into more detail about proving yet.

You can use ProB to animate contexts, too. Just right-click on the context in the explorer and select Start Animation / Model Checking. If ProB finds solutions for the specified constants that fulfil the axioms, an event "SETUP_CONTEXT" is enabled that assigns values to the constants. In our example, ProB should find a solution where Agatha is the murderer. You can actually inspect the axioms and the theorem in the state view to see why they are fulfilled.

This contribution requires the **ProB** plugin. The content is maintained by the plugin contributors and may be out of date.

This concludes the tutorial about contexts. The following section shows the complete Context.

2.6.3 The Final Context

CONTEXT agatha
SETS
    persons
CONSTANTS
    Agatha
    butler
    Charles
    hates
    richer
    killer
AXIOMS
    person_partition : $partition(persons, \{Agatha\}, \{butler\}, \{Charles\})$
    hate_relation : $hates \in persons \leftrightarrow persons$
    richer_relation : $richer \in persons \leftrightarrow persons \,\wedge$
                  $richer \cap id = \varnothing \,\wedge$
                  $(\forall x, y, z \cdot (x \mapsto y \in richer \wedge y \mapsto z \in richer)$
                      $\Rightarrow x \mapsto z \in richer) \,\wedge$
                  $(\forall x, y \cdot x \in persons \wedge y \in persons \wedge x \neq y$
                      $\Rightarrow (x \mapsto y \in richer \Leftrightarrow y \mapsto x \notin richer))$
    killer_type : $killer \in persons$
    killer_hates : $killer \mapsto Agatha \in hates$
    killer_not_richer : $killer \mapsto Agatha \notin richer$

charles_hates : $hates[\{Agatha\}] \cap hates[\{Charles\}] = \varnothing$

agatha_hates : $hates[\{Agatha\}] = persons \setminus \{butler\}$

butler_hates_1 : $\forall x \cdot (x \mapsto Agatha \notin richer$
$\Rightarrow butler \mapsto x \in hates)$

butler_hates_2 : $hates[\{Agatha\}] \subseteq hates[\{butler\}] \wedge$
$(\forall x \cdot x \in persons \Rightarrow hates[\{x\}] \neq persons)$

noone_hates_everyone : $\forall x \cdot x \in persons \wedge hates[\{x\}] \neq persons$

solution : $\boxed{\text{theorem}}$ $killer = Agatha$

END

2.7 Event-B Concepts

✓ **Goals:** This section is an overview of the fundamental concepts of Event-B.

In Event-B we have two kind of components. A *context* describes the static elements of a model. A *machine* describes the dynamic behavior of a model. We have already used a machine to model the traffic light problem in Section 2.4. In the last section (2.6), we used a context to model the Agatha problem.

2.7.1 Contexts

A context has the following components:

Sets User-defined types can be declared in the *SETS* section (see Section 3.3.4 for more information).

Constants We can declare constants here. The type of each constant must be declared in the axiom section.

Axioms The axiom section contains a list of predicates (called axioms). These axioms define rules that will always be the case for given elements of the context. These rules can then be taken for granted when developing a model. The axioms can be used later in proofs that for components that use (*"see"*) this context. Each axiom has a label attached to it.

Theorems Axioms can be marked as *theorems*. If this is the case, we are declaring that the predicate can be proved by using the axioms that have been written before this theorem. Once they have been proven, theorems can be used later in proofs just like the other axioms.

Extends A context may extend an arbitrary number of other contexts. When we extend another context A, we can then use all constants and axioms declared in A and also add new constants and axioms.

Rodin automatically generates *proof obligations* (often abbreviated as PO) for properties that need to be proven. Each proof obligation has a name that identifies where the proof obligation was generated. There are two kind of proof obligations generated in a context:

- Each theorem must be proven. The proof obligation's name has the form label/THM, where label is the theorem's label.

- Some expressions are not obviously *well-defined*. For example, the axiom $x \div y > 2$ is only meaningful if y is different from 0. Thus Rodin generates the proof obligation $y \neq 0$. A proof obligation for proving than an expression is well-defined has the name label/WD.

The order of the axioms and theorems matter because the proof of a theorem or the degree to which an expression is well-defined may depend on the axioms and theorems that have already been written. This is necessary to avoid circular reasoning.

2.7.2   Machines

A machine describes the dynamic behavior of a model by means of variables whose values are changed by events. A central aspect of modelling a machine is to prove that the machine never reaches an invalid state, i.e. the variables always have values that satisfy the invariants. Here is a brief summary of the part that a machine contains:

Refines A machine has the option of refining another one. We will see in Section 2.7.4 what that means.

Sees We can use the context's sets, constants and axioms in a machine by declaring it in the *Sees* section. The axioms can be used in every proof in the machine as hypotheses.

Variables The variables' values are determined by an initialisation event and can be changed by events. This constitutes the state of the machine. The type of each variable must be declared in the invariant section.

Invariants These are predicates that should be true for every reachable state. Each invariant has a label.

Events An event can assign new values to variables. The *guards* of an event specify the conditions under which it can be executed. The initialisation of the machine is a special case of an event.

2.7.3   Events

We saw in Section 2.4 what an event basically looks like by using the example of a traffic light:

Event   *set_cars* $\widehat{=}$
> **any**
>> *new_value*
>
> **where**
>> grd1 : *new_value* $\in BOOL$
>
> **then**
>> act1 : *cars_go* := *new_value*
>
> **end**

We have the event's name *set_cars*, a *parameter* with the name *new_value*, a *guard* with label grd1 and an *action* with label act1. An event can have an arbitrary number of parameters, guards and events.

The guards specify *when* an event is allowed to occur, i.e. the event can only be executed if the values of the machine's variables and parameters match the values listed in the guard. If this is the case, we say that the event is enabled. The actions describe *what* changes will then be applied to the variables.

Only the variables that are explicitly mentioned in the actions are affected. All the other variables keep their old values. Beside the simple assignment (:=), there are other forms of actions ($:\in$ or :|) which are explained in Section 3.2.4.

The *initialisation* of the machine is a special form of event. It has neither parameters nor guards.

Invariants must always be valid. To verify this, we must prove two things:

- The initialisation leads to a state where the invariant is valid.

- Assuming that the machine is in a state where the invariant is valid, every enabled event leads to a state where the invariant is valid.

Rodin generates proof obligations for every invariant that can be affected by an event, i.e. the invariant contains variables that can be changed by an event. The name of the proof obligation is then
event_name/invariant_label/INV. The goal of such a proof is to assert that when all affected variables are replaced by new values from the actions, the invariant still holds. The hypotheses for such a proof obligation consist of:

- All invariants, because we assume that all invariants hold before the event is triggered,

- All guards, because events can only be triggered when the guards are valid.

In the special case of an initialisation event, we cannot use the invariants because we do not make any assumptions about uninitialized machines.

2.7.4   Refinement

Refinement is a central concept in Event-B. Refinements are used to gradually introduce the details and complexity into a model. If a machine B refines a machine A, B can only behave in a way that corresponds to the behavior of A. We will now look into more detail of what "corresponds" here means. In such a setting, we call A the abstract and B the concrete machine.

This is just overview over the concept of refinement. Later in Section 2.8 we will use refinement in an example.

The concrete machine has its own set of variables. Its invariants can refer to the variables of the concrete and the abstract machine. If a invariant refers to both, we call it a "gluing invariant". The gluing invariants are used to relate the states between the concrete and abstract machines.

An event of the abstract machine may be refined by one or several events of the concrete machine. To ensure that the concrete machine does only what is allowed to do by the abstract one, we must prove two things:

- The concrete events can only occur when the abstract one occurs.

- If a concrete event occurs, the abstract event can occur in such a way that the resulting states correspond again, i.e. the gluing invariant remains true.

The first condition is called "guard strengthening". The resulting proof obligation has the label concrete_event/abstract_guard/GRD. We have to prove that under the assumption that the concrete event is enabled (i.e. its guard are true) and the invariants (both the abstract and the concrete) hold, the abstract guards holds as well. Thus the goal is to prove that the abstract guard, the invariants and the concrete guards can be used as hypotheses in the proof.

The second condition, that the gluing invariant remains true, is just a more general case of the proof obligation which ensures that an event does not violate the invariant. So the proof obligation's label is again concrete_event/concrete_invariant/INV. The goal is to prove that the invariant of the concrete machine is valid when each occurrence of a modified variable is replaced by its new value. The hypotheses we use are:

- We assume that the invariant of both the concrete and abstract machines were valid before the event occurred.

- The abstract invariants where the modified variables are replaced by their new values are valid because we know that the abstract event does not violate any invariants.

- The event occurs only when the guards of both the concrete and abstract machines are true.

These two conditions are the central issues that we need to deal with to prove the correctness of a refinement. We now just explain a few common special cases.

Variable re-use

Most of the time, we do not want to replace all variables with new ones. It is sometimes useful to keep all of the variables. We can do this just by repeating the names of the abstract variables in the variable section of the concrete machine. In that case, we must prove for each concrete event that changes this variable that the corresponding abstract event updates the variable in the same way. The proof obligation has the name concrete_event/abstract_action/SIM.

Introducing new events

An event in the concrete machine might not refine any event in the abstract machine. In that case it is assumed to refine *skip*, which is the event that does nothing and can occur any time. The guard strengthening is then true and doesn't need to be proven. We still have to prove that the gluing invariant holds but this time under the assumption that the abstract machine's variables have not changed. Therefore, the new state of our newly introduced event corresponds to the same state of our abstract machine from before the event happened.

Witnesses

Let's consider a situation where we have an abstract event with a parameter p and we are dealing with a refined event that no longer needs that parameter. We saw above that we have to prove that for each concrete event the abstract event may act accordingly. With the parameter, however, we now have the situation in which we must prove the existence of a value for p such that an abstract event exists. Proofs with existential quantification are often hard to do, so Event-b uses the a *witness* construct. A witness is just a predicate of the abstract parameter with the name of the variable as label. Often a witness has just the simple form $p = \ldots$, where $\ldots$ represents an expression that maps to p. How this works in practice is shown in Section 2.8.5.

2.8 Expanding the Traffic Light System: Contexts and Refinement

 Goals: We apply what we learned in the previous section by introducing a context with traffic light colours and a refinement to integrate them. We will also introduce another refinement for the push buttons.

2.8.1 Data Refinement

We will continue the example from Section 2.4, where we built a simplified model of a traffic light controller. The model was simplified because we abstracted the traffic lights to TRUE and FALSE and a number of features were still missing.

We will introduce data refinement in this section. The objective is to create a mapping between the abstract traffic light values and actual colours. Figure 2.13 depicts our mapping for the traffic light.

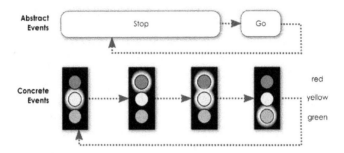

Figure 2.13: Mapping between Abstract and Concrete Events

For simplicity, the traffic light for pedestrians consists of only two lights: red and green.

We break this problem into two steps:

1. Create a context with the data structures for the colours.

2. Create a refinement of the existing model that sees the new context and refines the boolean states into colours.

2.8.2   A Context with Colours

Start by creating a context called `ctx1`, as described in Section 2.6. We model the colours of the traffic light as a so-called "enumerated set" (3.3.4): We explicitly specify all elements (the three colours) of a new user-defined data type. We define the constants:

 CONSTANTS
            red
            yellow
            green

We introduce the new data type as a set:

 SETS
            COLOURS

And last, we need to provide typing of the constants. We do this by creating a partition (3.3.4):

 AXIOMS

$$type : partition(COLOURS, \{red\}, \{yellow\}, \{green\})$$

 Please note the curly braces {} around the colours. It's very easy to forget these, but if they are missing, typing errors will be displayed that are very hard for a novice to interpret.

This completes the context.

2.8.3 The Actual Data Refinement

The easiest way to create a refinement is by right-clicking on the machine in the project browser and selecting Refine (in this case, we will be refining the machine mac from the project tutorial-3). This will create a "stub" consisting of all variables and events. Please use this method to create a machine with name mac1.

When you have refined a machine, the Rodin Editor will show you all the elements of the abstracted machine, but the inherited actions will be shown in grey. This means that you can add actions to the event, but you cannot edit the actions that are already there.

 For this tutorial, make sure that you right-click on the machine and select refine from the drop-down menu. If you have created a machine the normal way and later edited the refines section, the tutorial will assume that you have events (e.g. set_peds_go) and variables that you do not have.

First we have to make the machine aware of the context by adding a sees (3.2.4) statement. To do this, place your cursor to the left of the small green arrow ( ) next to your machine name mac1. Right click and select Add Child ⟩ Event-B Sees Context Relationship. A SEES heading will appear with the value –undefined–. Place your cursor over the undefined section and click. A small box listing all of the contexts in the project will pop up. Select ctx1:

MACHINE mac1
REFINES mac
SEES ctx1

We will start with the traffic lights for the pedestrians. It has only two colours (red and green) and only one of them is shown at a time. We introduce a new variable called peds_colour to represent which of the lights is shown. The variable has a corresponding invariant and initialisation (the changes are shown in the following code snippet). The *extended* keyword in the initialisation means that all actions from the refined initialisation are copied:

VARIABLES
    peds_colour

INVARIANTS
  inv4 : $peds\_colour \in \{red, green\}$
EVENTS
Initialisation
  extended
  begin
    init4 : $peds\_colour := red$
  end
END

Next, we will create a gluing invariant (3.2.4) that associates peds_go from the abstract machine with the variable peds_colour that we just created. The gluing invariant will map TRUE to green and FALSE to red:

 INVARIANTS
  gluing : $peds\_go = TRUE \Leftrightarrow peds\_colour = green$

In its current state, this gluing invariant can be violated: if the event set_peds_go is triggered, for instance, the variable peds_go will change but peds_colour will not. We expect that this will result in undischarged proof obligations (3.2.7). We can check this by expanding the machine in the Event-B Explorer. Indeed, we now see two undischarged proof obligations (compare with Figure 2.14).

▾ Ⓜ,mac1
  ▸ ○ Variables
  ▸ ⟡, Invariants
  ▸ ✳, Events
  ▾ ⓘ Proof Obligations
      🅐ᴬINITIALISATION/inv4/INV
      🅐ᴬINITIALISATION/gluing/INV
      🅐ᴬset_peds_go/gluing/INV
      🅐ᴬset_peds_stop/gluing/INV

Figure 2.14: Mapping between Abstract and Concrete Events

To fix this, we have to modify the two events in question. Let's start with set_peds_go. First, we change the event from extended to not extended in the Editor by placing our cursor over the keyword extended and clicking. This is shown in Figure 2.15.

This change will copy the guard and action from the abstract machine, so that we can modify it. We can now replace the action with the corresponding action regarding peds_colour (replacing peds_go := true with peds_colour := green).

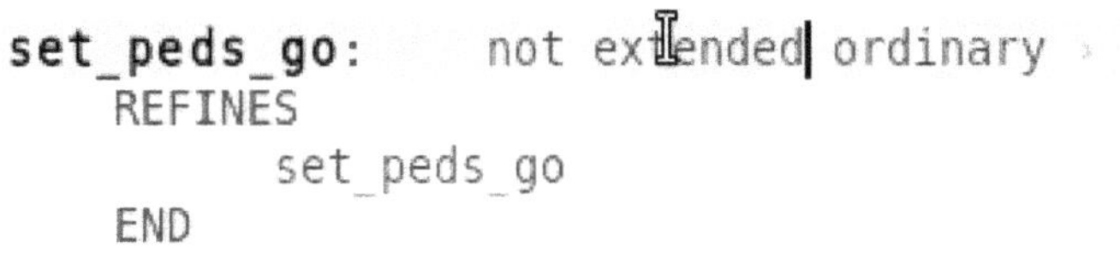

set_peds_go: not extended| ordinary
    REFINES
        set_peds_go
  END

Figure 2.15: Switch from extended to not extended

While we are at it, we can also rename the name of the event to something more fitting (e.g. set_peds_green).

Next, we perform the corresponding change on set_peds_stop (change the action to peds_colour := red and rename the event set_peds_red). Lastly, the event set_cars also contains a reference to peds_go that must be replaced (in the second guard, replace peds_go = FALSE with peds_colour = red).

Once all references to peds_go have been replace, we can remove the variable peds_go from the VARIABLES section. You will also need to change the INITIALISATION event to not extended and remove the action which initialises the variable peds_go. Now you shouldn't have any errors or warnings, and all proof obligations should be discharged.

⚠ If you get the error message "Identifier peds_go has not been declared", then there are references to the refined variable left somewhere in the model.

2.8.4 The refined machine with data refinement for peds_go

MACHINE mac1
REFINES mac
SEES ctx1
VARIABLES
    cars_go
    peds_colour
INVARIANTS
    inv4 : $peds\_colour \in \{red, green\}$
    gluing : $peds\_go = TRUE \Leftrightarrow peds\_colour = green$
EVENTS
Initialisation
    begin
        act1 : $cars\_go := FALSE$
        init4 : $peds\_colour := red$
    end
Event $set\_peds\_green \mathrel{\widehat{=}}$
refines set_peds_go
    when

> $\quad$ grd1 : $cars\_go = FALSE$
> **then**
> $\qquad$ act2 : $peds\_colour := green$
> **end**

Event $set\_peds\_red \;\widehat{=}$
refines set_peds_stop
> **begin**
> $\qquad$ act1 : $peds\_colour := red$
> **end**

Event $set\_cars \;\widehat{=}$
refines set_cars
> **any**
> $\qquad new\_value$
> **where**
> $\qquad$ grd1 : $new\_value \in BOOL$
> $\qquad$ grd2 : $new\_value = TRUE \Rightarrow peds\_colour = red$
> **then**
> $\qquad$ act1 : $cars\_go := new\_value$
> **end**

END

2.8.5   Witnesses

The refinement of set_cars is more difficult since the event uses a parameter (the new value for cars_go). In order to refine it, we need a witness (3.2.4).

A witness is to an event's parameter what a gluing invariant is to a variable: it is a mapping between the abstract parameter and the new parameter and allows the abstract parameter to disappear. In this example, the abstract parameter new_value is of type BOOL, and we introduce a new parameter new_value_colours of type COLOURS.

 The naming of a witnesses' label is extremely important. It must be the name of the abstract parameter. In our example, the label must be new_value

Let's get started. We first provide the new variable, gluing invariant, typing invariant and initialisation as we have done before (at this point you can also rename the gluing invariant from the last section as gluing_peds in order to be able to determine between the two gluing invariants). Note that the traffic light for the cars can show more than one colour at a time. Therefore, the variable contains a set of colours instead of just one colour (as modelled for peds_colour):

 VARIABLES
> cars_colours

INVARIANTS
> inv5 : $cars\_colours \subseteq COLOURS$

> gluing_cars : $cars\_go = TRUE \Leftrightarrow green \in cars\_colours$

EVENTS
Initialisation
>   **begin**
>>   init5 : $cars\_colours := \{red\}$
>   **end**
END

We also have to modify the guard on set_peds_green, which is something that you should now be able to figure out yourself (just replace cars_go = FALSE with green $\notin$ cars_colours).

The interesting piece is the last event, set_cars, which we rename as set_cars-_colours. We change the parameter to new_value_colours and type it as a subset of COLOURS.

The witness appears in the with section of the event. The label **must** be new_value. The value itself must describe the relationship between the abstract parameter new_value and the new parameter new_value_colours. As we use the parameter as the new value for the variable cars_colours, the witness is an adaptation of the gluing invariant (we just replace cars_colours with new_value_colours).

In most cases, the witness is a slightly modified gluing invariant.

Here is the resulting event:

Event $set\_cars\_colours \,\widehat{=}$
refines set_cars
>   **any**
>> $new\_value\_colours$
>   **where**
>>   grd1 : $new\_value\_colours \subseteq COLOURS$
>>   grd2 : $green \in new\_value\_colours \Rightarrow peds\_colour = red$
>   **with**
>>   new_value : **new_value** = TRUE$\Leftrightarrow$**green** $\in$ **new_value_colours**
>   **then**
>>   act1 : $cars\_colours := new\_value\_colours$
>   **end**

Now you can get rid of the variable cars_go and its initialisation clause, and there will not be any errors or warnings. But even though all proof obligations are now discharged, we're not done yet. Even though the traffic light doesn't violate the safety property from the abstract machine, it doesn't behave the way described in Section 2.8.1. We still have to ensure that the lights are activated in the proper sequence. We can impose this behavior by adding four guards each of which define one transition:

$\text{grd\_y\_r}:$ $cars\_colours = \{yellow\} \Rightarrow new\_value\_colours = \{red\}$

$\text{grd\_r\_ry}:$ $cars\_colours = \{red\} \Rightarrow new\_value\_colours = \{red, yellow\}$

$\text{grd\_ry\_g}:$ $cars\_colours = \{red, yellow\} \Rightarrow new\_value\_colours = \{green\}$

$\text{grd\_g\_y}:$ $cars\_colours = \{green\} \Rightarrow new\_value\_colours = \{yellow\}$

2.8.6   Discussion

Notice that we have used two very different approaches to model the traffic lights for cars and pedestrians. For the pedestrians, we created one event for each state transition. For the cars, we handled all states in one single event.

You will often be confronted with situations where many modelling approaches are possible. You should consider two main factors when modelling: (1) the readability of the model and (2) the ease of the proof. In this case, both approaches are equally good (although we wouldn't recommend mixing different approaches in one model. We did it here only to demonstrate both approaches).

We will cover deadlocks later in Section 2.10.1. If you are interested in the topic, it may interest you to examine the traffic light model for deadlocks. Consider cars_colours = { green, red }. This is a legal state, but it would block set_cars_colours forever. A model checker (such as ProB) could find it. In this case, however, this is not a problem because with the given initialisation and events this state is not reachable in the first place.

We hope that this section helped you to understand the power of abstraction. The safety invariant $\neg(cars\_go = TRUE \wedge peds\_go = TRUE)$ from Section 2.4.4 was very simple. We could now introduce colours because we are confident that the invariant will still be valid (assuming, of course, that our gluing invariant is correct).

2.8.7   The Refined Machine with All Data Refinement

MACHINE mac1
REFINES mac
SEES ctx1
VARIABLES
    peds_colour
    cars_colours
INVARIANTS
    inv4 : $peds\_colour \in \{red, green\}$
    inv5 : $cars\_colours \subseteq COLOURS$
    gluing_peds : $peds\_go = TRUE \Leftrightarrow peds\_colour = green$
    gluing_cars : $cars\_go = TRUE \Leftrightarrow green \in cars\_colours$
EVENTS
Initialisation
    begin
        init4 : $peds\_colour := red$

init5 : $cars\_colours := \{red\}$
    end
Event $set\_peds\_green \; \widehat{=}$
refines *set_peds_go*
    when
        grd1 : $green \notin cars\_colours$
    then
        act2 : $peds\_colour := green$
    end
Event $set\_peds\_red \; \widehat{=}$
refines *set_peds_stop*
    begin
        act1 : $peds\_colour := red$
    end
Event $set\_cars\_colours \; \widehat{=}$
refines *set_cars*
    any
        $new\_value\_colours$
    where
        grd1 : $new\_value\_colours \subseteq COLOURS$
        grd2 : $green \in new\_value\_colours \Rightarrow peds\_colour = red$
        grd_y_r : $cars\_colours = \{yellow\} \Rightarrow new\_value\_colours = \{red\}$
        grd_r_ry : $cars\_colours = \{red\} \Rightarrow new\_value\_colours = \{red, yellow\}$
        grd_ry_g : $cars\_colours = \{red, yellow\} \Rightarrow new\_value\_colours = \{green\}$
        grd_g_y : $cars\_colours = \{green\} \Rightarrow new\_value\_colours = \{yellow\}$
    with
        new_value : $\mathbf{new\_value} = \mathrm{TRUE} \Leftrightarrow green \in \mathbf{new\_value\_colours}$
    then
        act1 : $cars\_colours := new\_value\_colours$
    end
END

2.8.8   One more Refinement: The Push Button

We will demonstrate another application of refinement: introducing new features into an existing model. A typical traffic light system allows the pedestrians to request a light change by pressing a button. We will introduce this feature in a new refinement.

We could have introduced the push button in the initial machine, but introducing it later allows us to structure the model and makes it easier to understand and navigate.

We will realize this feature by introducing a new boolean variable for the push button. We will introduce an event that notifies the model that a push

button has been pressed. Upon allowing the pedestrians to cross, we will reset
the push button. This is a simplification of the problem. In practice, a lot would
depend on the controller's capabilities. We would have to consider things like
how the push button notification gets to the controller software and how the
pressing/depressing sequence is handled. In this example, the event directly
sets the controller's state. This demonstrates the concept of feature refinement
without introducing too much complexity for a tutorial example.

As in the previous section, we create a new refinement mac2 by right-clicking
on mac1 and selecting Refine. A stub is generated that contains the events
from the abstract machine. We simply add a new variable for the push button
(including typing and an initialisation clause). We also introduce an event that
sets the button. This event doesn't work while the pedestrians have a green
light.

VARIABLES
    button
INVARIANTS
    type_button : $button \in BOOL$
EVENTS
Initialisation
    extended
    begin
        init_button : $button := FALSE$
    end
Event *push_button* $\widehat{=}$
    when
        grd : $peds\_colour = red$
    then
        act : $button := TRUE$
    end
END

Now we need to integrate the push button with the traffic light logic:

- Upon pressing the button, the pedestrians must eventually get a green
  light.

- At some point, the button variable must be reset.

As we will see in the following discussion, this be more tricky than it first
appears. For now, we will introduce a guard preventing the car lights from
turning green when the button is true, and we will reset the button when the
pedestrian lights turn red:

Event *set_peds_red* $\widehat{=}$
    extends *set_peds_red*
        begin

$$\texttt{act\_button} : \mathit{button} := \mathit{FALSE}$$
     end
Event $\mathit{set\_cars\_colours} \mathrel{\widehat{=}}$
extends $\mathit{set\_cars\_colours}$
     where
           $\texttt{grd\_button} : \neg(\mathit{cars\_colours} = \{\mathit{red}\} \wedge \mathit{button} = \mathit{TRUE})$
     end

2.8.9 Discussion

There are a number of problems associated with the model in its current state. Let's start with how the button is reset: The way we built our model so far, set_peds_red can be triggered at any time; there is not a single guard which prevents this. Therefore, the button could be reset any time without the pedestrian light ever turning green.

This could be prevented with additional guards. For instance, the traffic light events could require an actual change in the light's status. This in turn could lead to deadlocks.

But even if we introduce such guards, we could get stuck in a situation where cars would never get green light any more. Consider the following scenario: (1) pedestrians get green light; (2) the light turns red; (3) a pedestrian presses the button again; (4) this prevents the car lights from turning green. Instead, the pedestrians get a green light again and the cycle continues.

There are tactics to address all these issues. However, it is rarely possible to generate proof obligations for such scenarios (without making the model much more complicated). It can be useful to use model checkers to validate the model's behaviour or even to use temporal logic to articulate properties of the model.

 As an exercise, try to improve the model to address these issues.

2.9 Proving

 Goals: The goal of this section is to get familiar with the Proving Perspective and to carry out a simple proof by hand. It also introduces more sophisticated data structures than the ones we introduced so far.

2.9.1 The Celebrity Problem

In this section, we will work with the model of the so-called celebrity problem.

 We are using a new model instead of the traffic light because it provides us with some proofs where manual interaction is necessary.

In the setting for this problem, we have a "knows" relation between persons. This relation is defined so that

- no one knows himself,

- the celebrity knows nobody,

- everybody knows the celebrity.

The problem's goal is to find the celebrity. We want to model an algorithm that fulfills this task.

2.9.2 Importing a project

Rather than creating the model step by step, we have provided the model as an archive file.

 Make sure that you have no existing Project named "Celebrity", before importing the project. If you have, then rename it by right clicking the project and selecting Rename...

Import the archive file Celebrity.zip[6] to your Event-B Explorer. To do this, select File 〉 Import 〉 General 〉 Existing Projects into Workspace. Then select the option to import an existing archive file. Use the browse function to find your archive file and import it. After you have selected the appropriate archive file, click on Finish.

It will take a few seconds for Rodin to extract and load all the files. Once this is done, a few problems will be displayed in the Rodin Problems view (compare with Figure 2.16).

Rodin Problems ⊠ ☐ Properties ⏑ Tasks		
0 errors, 5 warnings, 0 infos		
Description ∧	Resource	Path
▽ ⬚ Warnings (5 items)		
ⓘ Abstract event celebrity not refined, although not disabled	Celebrity_1.bum	Celebrity
ⓘ Inconsistent use of event label celebrity	Celebrity_1.bum	Celebrity
ⓘ Witness for x missing. Default witness generated	Celebrity_2.bum	Celebrity
ⓘ Witness for y missing. Default witness generated	Celebrity_2.bum	Celebrity
ⓘ Witness for y missing. Default witness generated	Celebrity_2.bum	Celebrity

Figure 2.16: Warnings in the Rodin Problems View

We will describe how the model is organized below in Section 2.9.5. But before we do so, we will fix the existing problems.

---

[6]The URL of the resource is: http://handbook.event-b.org/current/files/Celebrity.zip

2.9.3   Fixing Problems

Before proceeding, we will fix the problems shown in Figure 2.16. Let's take a look at the warning stating that the event label "celebrity" is misused ("Inconsistent use of event label celebrity"). Double-click on this warning to open the Celebrity_1 machine. The line with the error is already underlined in yellow[7]. This error is produced by the event called celebrity.

The problem is that the event is not declared as a refinement. To solve the problem, add an Event-B Refines Event Relationship child which will add a new entry in the REFINES section. To do so, right-click in the empty space to the left of the word celebrity or place your cursor directly to the left of the small green arrow ( ) and right-click. Now select Add Child ⟩ Event-B Refines Event Relationship.

> ⚠ Make sure that the cursor is on the correct line before right-clicking. Otherwise, you will get the wrong context menu. Also, make sure that you are not in "text edit" mode (e.g. clicking on a word like "celebrity" that you can edit will bring you into "text edit" mode). This will give you the wrong context menu as well. See the FAQ for more info (4.3.12).

This declares that the event is a refinement of an event with the same name in the abstract machine (3.2.4). This is the case here, so we can now save the project and the warning should disappear.

The three remaining warnings state that witnesses (3.2.4) are missing. Double click on the warning to open the concrete model (here Celebrity_2). Then add an Event-B Witness child to the event called celebrity.

A default witness wit1 has been created, with a default value ⊤ (e.g. the predicate "true") which we need to change. The name of a witness has to be the same as the parameter of the corresponding abstract event that it is refining. Here the name of the witness will have to be x so that it can be a witness for the parameter x of the corresponding abstract event in the machine Celebrity_1. The abstract event has the assignment $r := x$, while the concrete one has the assignment $r := b$. So the content of the witness should $b = x$. The event should now look as follows:

Event   *celebrity* $\widehat{=}$
   refines   *celebrity*
      when
         grd1 : $R = \varnothing$
      with
         x : $b = x$
      then
         act1 : $r := b$
      end

---

[7]This is the behaviour of the default editor. Other editors may exhibit a different behaviour

Edit the content and save the file. One warning will disappear, and only two will remain.

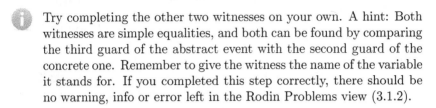 Try completing the other two witnesses on your own. A hint: Both witnesses are simple equalities, and both can be found by comparing the third guard of the abstract event with the second guard of the concrete one. Remember to give the witness the name of the variable it stands for. If you completed this step correctly, there should be no warning, info or error left in the Rodin Problems view (3.1.2).

The following section (2.9.4) shows the corrected Celebrity_2 machine.

2.9.4 The Final Second Refinement

MACHINE Celebrity_2
REFINES Celebrity_1
SEES Celebrity_c0
VARIABLES
    r
    R
    b
INVARIANTS
    inv1 : $R \subseteq P$
    inv2 : $b \in P$
    inv3 : $b \notin R$
    inv4 : $Q = R \cup \{b\}$
EVENTS
Initialisation
    begin
        act1 : $r :\in P$
        act2 : $b, R : |b' \in P \wedge R' = P \setminus \{b'\}$
    end
Event *celebrity* $\widehat{=}$
refines *celebrity*
    when
        grd1 : $R = \varnothing$
    with
        x : $b = x$
    then
        act1 : $r := b$
    end
Event *remove_1* $\widehat{=}$
refines *remove_1*
    any
        x
    where

$$\text{grd1} : x \in R$$
$$\text{grd2} : x \mapsto b \in k$$

with

$$\text{y} : \text{b} = \text{y}$$

then

$$\text{act1} : R := R \setminus \{x\}$$

end

Event *remove_2* $\widehat{=}$
refines *remove_2*

any

$$x$$

where

$$\text{grd1} : x \in R$$
$$\text{grd2} : x \mapsto b \notin k$$

with

$$\text{y} : \text{b} = \text{y}$$

then

$$\text{act2} : b := x$$
$$\text{act1} : R := R \setminus \{x\}$$

end

END

2.9.5 The Celebrity algorithm

We will now take a brief tour through the model to see how the problem and algorithm are specified. The celebrity problem itself is described in the context Celebrity_c0. There are three constants. P is the set of persons, each represented by a number, c is the celebrity we are looking for and k is the "knows" relation between the persons. The axioms encode the properties about the "knows" relation that we stated above.

CONTEXT Celebrity_c0
CONSTANTS

    k

    c

    P

AXIOMS

$$\text{axm1} : P \subseteq \mathbb{N}$$
$$\text{axm2} : c \in P$$
$$\text{axm3} : k \in (P \setminus \{c\}) \leftrightarrow P$$
$$\text{axm4} : k^{-1}[\{c\}] = P \setminus \{c\}$$
$$\text{axm5} : k \cap id = \varnothing$$

END

In the most abstract machine Celebrity_0 we specify what the algorithm should do. The variable r can be any person initially and the event celebrity

finds the celebrity in one step. After the event `celebrity` has occurred, r
contains the result of the algorithm. You might then wonder why there is a
problem if you can just pick the celebrity and assign it to the result. This is
because we defined our problem in such a way so that we are certain a celebrity
c exists and the algorithm simply returns it. Later in the refinement, we will
model how to find the celebrity without using c. Because of the refinement
relation, we know that the algorithm works correctly.

MACHINE   Celebrity_0
SEES   Celebrity_c0
VARIABLES
    r
INVARIANTS
    inv1 : $r \in P$
EVENTS
Initialisation
    begin
        act1 : $r :\in P$
    end
Event   *celebrity* $\widehat{=}$
    begin
        act1 : $r := c$
    end
END

So let's have a look at the first refinement `Celebrity_1`. A variable Q is
introduced which contains a subset of the persons, the potential celebrities. We
start with Q being all persons. Two new events, `remove_1` and `remove_2`, are
added to remove people from Q who cannot be the celebrity. `remove_1` removes
a person that knows somebody while `remove_2` removes a person that is not
known by any other person. An invariants states that the celebrity is always
in Q. When there is just one person left in the set, we know that this is the
celebrity.

The second refinement, `Celebrity_2`, then splits the potential celebrities Q
into one arbitrary person – the candidate b – and the "rest" R. `remove_1` then
removes a person x from R if b knows x. `remove_2` checks if there is a person
x in R that does not know the candidate. If found, x is the new candidate b
and is removed from the rest R. If R is empty, we know that the candidate is
the celebrity. (We do not show the machine here because it simply takes up too
much space — please consult the project that you imported earlier to inspect
the model.)

The third refinement then makes some more assumptions about the given
problem. The context `Celebrity_c1` extends `Celebrity_c0` and states that
there are $n + 1$ persons with the numbers $0 .. n$.

CONTEXT   Celebrity_c1

EXTENDS Celebrity_c0
CONSTANTS
   n
AXIOMS
   axm1 : $n \in \mathbb{N}$
   axm2 : $n > 0$
   axm3 : $P = 0 .. n$
END

Instead of having an abstract data structure like a set, the third refinement just introduces an index variable a that points to the first person of R, which is the group of people who have not yet been checked. Instead of taking an arbitrary element from R as in the second refinement, the remove events just takes the first element a. a is then removed from R by increasing it by one. When a is larger then n, R is empty and b contains the result.

This last refinement works only on the following three integer variables: The index a, the candidate b and the result r. Each event is deterministic and in every step only one event is enabled. The events together can be interpreted as an implementation of the algorithm:

$r := 0$	// initialisation `act1`
$a := 1$	// initialisation `act2`
$b := 0$	// initialisation `act3`
while $a \leq n$ **do**	// guard in `remove_1` and `remove_2`
if $a \mapsto b \in k$ **then**	// guard in `remove_1` and negated in `remove_2`
$a := a + 1$	// action in `remove_1`
else	// $a \mapsto b \notin k$
$b := a$	// action `act1` in `remove_2`
$a := a + 1$	// action `act2` in `remove_2`
end if	
end while	
$r := b$	// action in `celebrity`

2.9.6   The First Proof

In this section, we will carry out proofs for the model of the Celebrity Problem. To do this, click on the box in the upper right hand corner that has a little plus sign and switch to the Proving Perspective. You can switch between perspectives using the shortcut bar as shown in Figure 2.17.

 If the Proving Perspective is not available in the menu, select Other... 〉 Proving. This will open a new window which shows all available perspectives.

We should now see the window in Figure 2.18.
The **Proving Perspective** contains three new important views:

Figure 2.17: Switch Perspective

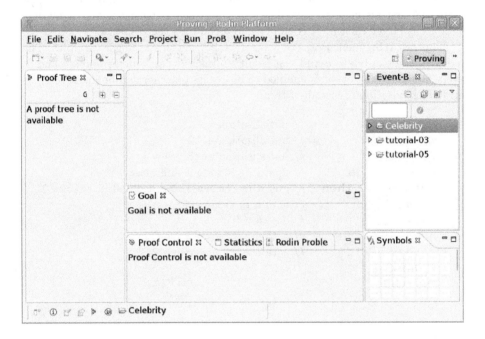

Figure 2.18: Rodin Proving Perspective

Proof Tree View (3.1.7) Here we see a tree of the proof that we have done so
far and the current position in it. By clicking in the tree, we can navigate
within the proof. We have not yet started the proof, so there is nothing
to see yet.

Proof Control View (3.1.7) This is where we perform interactive proofs.

Goal View (3.1.7) This window shows what needs to be proved at the current
position inside the proof tree.

Expand the `Celebrity_1` machine in the Event-B Explorer. Then expand the Proof Obligations section. We can see that the auto prover (3.1.7) did quite a good job. Only three proofs have not been completed[8] (a completed proof is indicated by a green mark ✅).

Each proof has a label, e.g. remove_1/inv2/INV. Proof labels are explained in Section 3.2.7.

Let's start with the proof remove_1/inv2/INV of `Celebrity_1`. To do this, double click on the proof obligation remove_1/inv2/INV. We should now see the window as shown in Figure 2.19.

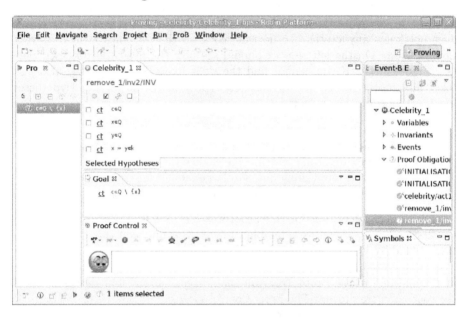

Figure 2.19: Proof Obligation

Make sure that you understand the different buttons in the Proof Control View (3.1.7).

Here we need to prove that the event **remove_1** preserves the invariant **inv2**, $c \in Q$. The event's action assigns the new value $Q \setminus \{x\}$ to Q. Because we know that invariant $c \in Q$ was valid before the assignment, it is sufficient to prove that we do not remove c from Q, i.e. $x \neq c$. Type this into the Proof Control View (3.1.7) and press the ᵃʰ button.

---

[8]Interestingly enough, this number can vary: Provers can be configured in the preferences and changes there can have an impact on the ability to automatically discharge proofs. In addition, all provers have timeouts. On a slow machine, some proof obligations may not be discharged whereas on a faster machine with the same timeout they would be discharged.

In order to undo a step, click on a node in the `Proof Tree View` and click on the ✂ button in the `Proof Control View` or open the context menu of a node and select **Prune**.

Take a look at the Proof Tree View. The root node should now be labelled with **ah** $(x \neq c)$, which is the hypothesis that we just added. This node has three children: The first proves that $x \neq c$ is well-defined[9], which is $\top$ and has already been trivially proven. The second is the proof of the hypotheses $\neg x = c$. The third is the proof of the original goal where the new hypotheses can be used.

The new goal is $\neg x = c$. Now, try selecting the right hypotheses by yourself in order to complete the proof (Hint: What axiom states that the celebrity does not know anybody?). To do this, click on the ☑ button in the `Proof Control View`. On the left side we should see now the Search Hypotheses view (see Figure 2.20). If you cannot find the right hypotheses, you may also just select all hypotheses. To add the selected hypothesis to the Selected Hypotheses View just click on the ✱ button.

There is usually no harm in selecting all hypothesis, but this approach is not optimal. By providing only necessary hypotheses and no more, we drastically increase the chance that the prover will find the solution before timing out. On large models it is next to impossible to prove everything without hand-picking the hypotheses.

The correct hypothesis for this proof was $k \in (P \setminus \{c\}) \leftrightarrow P$ (axiom 3 from the first context). If you were unable to figure this out, add this hypothesis to the selected hypothesis window now. Now click on the ᵖ⁰ button to prove the goal $\neg x = c$ with the Predicate prover on selected hypothesis. The goal should be discharged and in the Proof Tree you should see that the first two children of the root node are proven. The Proof Control View should now show the original goal $c \in Q \setminus x$ and $x \neq c$ is now one of our hypotheses.[10] Click a second time on the ᵖ⁰ button in order to finalize the proof. The smiley in the Proof Control View should now become green indicating that all sequents of the proof tree are discharged as shown in Figure 2.21.

After saving the proof, the proof obligation remove_1/inv2/INV in the Event-B Explorer should now have a ⊘ next to it.

Those proof obligations that were automatically discharged are marked with a tiny "A" next to the ⊘ . As the one we just discharged was proven manually, this is now the first discharged PO without an "A".

There are alternative ways to prove the proof obligation. For instance, we can use the ✏ button to load all hidden hypotheses that contain identifiers in common with the goal into the Selected Hypotheses View, and we can also use it with the selected hypotheses.

---

[9]You may wonder how we know that this is the well-definedness proof obligation

[10]The prover has rewritten this as $\neg x = c$

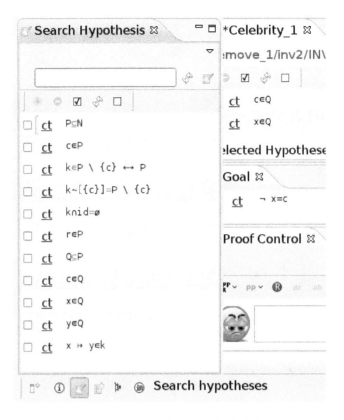

Figure 2.20: Search Hypothesis View

In order to move to the next undischarged proof obligation, you may also use the Next Undischarged PO button (⇨) of the Proof Control View (3.1.7). The next proof can be solved the same way as the last one.

As an exercise, try to prove Celebrity_2. A small hint: To do this, we have to fill in an existential quantifier. We need to instantiate b' correctly. The auto prover should have proved that $b' \in P$, so look for a variable that is already in P and add this value to the Selected Hypotheses View. To instantiate b', type the name of the variable you have chosen into the yellow box that is shown in the Goal View (3.1.7) and then click on the red existential quantifier. Now all open branches of the proof tree can be proved with the ᵖ⁰ prover. After this, we have completed all the proofs, and the model is ready for use.

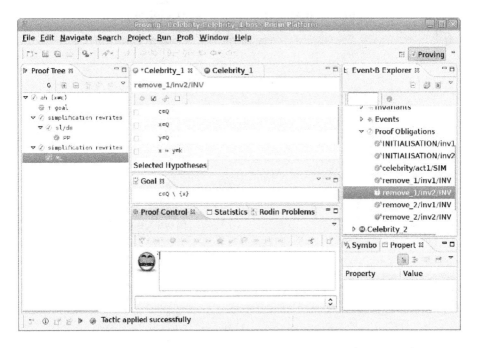

Figure 2.21: The green smiley indicates that all sequents of the proof tree are discharged

2.9.7   Proving — an Art or a Science?

Proving can be quite frustrating for both beginners and advanced users. Beginners sometimes get the impression that proving is just "clicking around" that sometimes works and sometimes does not. When it does work, it's not really clear why. The proof tree is also difficult to read even for experienced users. We provided some additional guidance on provers in the reference chapter (3.4.5) that may be of help, but keep in mind that proving is a skill that can only be learned by practice. Here we are trying to help you learn how you can use Rodin to solve proofs, but actually teaching you how to prove something is not really in the scope of this document.

2.10 Proving Deadlock Freeness

 Goals: In this section, we will take a closer look at a few more complex proofs. Here we use the model of a location access controller. The goal is to develop the proofs that ensure there are no deadlocks present in the initial model and in the first refinement.

 This example has been taken from the Event-B book (1.2.1) and is quite sophisticated. In this section, we are dealing with a subset of the complete model. We encourage readers to consult the example in the book.

Through the model used in this section, we study a complete system and mention the proof rules of formal development. This system's job is to control the access of certain people to different locations of a site. The system is thus based on whether a person has (or does not have) access to a particular location.

Before describing the initial model, import the archive file Doors.zip[11] that contains the model. To do this, select File ⟩ Import ⟩ General ⟩ Existing Project into Workspace. Then select the according archive file and click on Finish. It will take Rodin a few seconds to extract and load all the files.

2.10.1 Deadlock Freeness of initial model

Let us look at the initial model which consists of the context doors_ctx1 and the machine doors_0. There are two carrier sets in the model context. One is for people (P) and the other is for locations (L). There is a location called outside (*outside*) and a relation (*aut*) which defines the places that people are allowed to go. Everyone is permitted to go outside. The model machine has one event, pass, which changes the location of a person and one variable, *sit*, which denotes where a person is located.

Looking through the initial model, you will see that everything already has been proved (for the initial model and initial contexts). This is true, but Rodin has not yet proved that the model is deadlock free yet, so we will have to prove this ourselves. A model is considered to be deadlocked if the system reaches a state where there are no outgoing transitions. The objective of this section is to develop proofs for deadlock freeness for the initial model and for the first refinement.

Consider the event pass from the initial model:

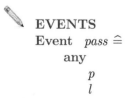 **EVENTS**
    Event   *pass* $\widehat{=}$
        any
            p
            l

---

[11]The URL of the resource is: http://handbook.event-b.org/current/files/Doors.zip

   where
       grd11 : $p \mapsto l \in aut$
       grd12 : $sit(p) \neq l$
   then
       act11 : $sit(p) := l$
   end
END

Since the initial model has only one event (pass), the system might deadlock when both guards of the event (grd11 and grd12) are false. In this case, to prove that no deadlocks can occur requires proving that someone can always change room. We must therefore prove that the two guards are always true. To do this, add a new derived invariant (a theorem) to doors_0 called DLF (click once on the label **not theorem** to make it switch to **theorem**) and change the predicate so that it is the conjunction of the two guards. The difference between a "normal" invariant and one that is marked as theorem is that you must prove that a theorem is always valid when the previously listed invariants are valid. Then we don't need to prove that an event preserves the invariant marked as theorem because we can conclude this logically when it already preserves the other invariants.

 INVARIANTS

   DLF : $\boxed{\text{theorem}}$ $\exists p, l \cdot (p \mapsto l \in aut \land sit(p) \neq l)$

 Make sure that when you add your DLF invariant, you add it after the other two invariants in doors_0. The auto prover uses these invariants to prove that the DLF invariant is well defined, and if they aren't in the right order, the proof obligation DLF/WD will not be discharged

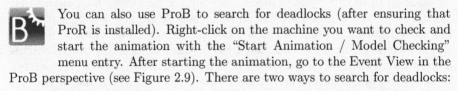 You can also use ProB to search for deadlocks (after ensuring that ProR is installed). Right-click on the machine you want to check and start the animation with the "Start Animation / Model Checking" menu entry. After starting the animation, go to the Event View in the ProB perspective (see Figure 2.9). There are two ways to search for deadlocks:

- Press the Check button and mark Find Deadlocks. Then start the model checking by pressing the button Start consistency checking. ProB then systematically "executes" all events and tries to find a state where no event is enabled.

- An alternative is to select Deadlock Freedom Checking after clicking on the triangle to the right of the Check button. ProB will then prompt you to input a predicate, but this is optional, so leave it blank. The difference with this alternative alternative is that ProB searches now for variable values where all the invariants are valid but none of the guards are valid.

This contribution requires the **ProB** plugin. The content is maintained by the plugin contributors and may be out of date.

Save the machine. We see in the Event-B Explorer View that the auto-prover (3.1.7) fails to prove the theorem DLF/THM.

 If you cannot find the proof obligation DLF/THM, maybe you forgot to mark the invariant as a theorem by clicking once on the **not theorem** label next to the invariant. Another reason that you might not see the proof obligation DLF/THM is that you have forgotten to rename the invariant "DLF".

Let us analyze whether this is an inconsistency in the model. Switch to the `Proving Perspective` and double click on the proof obligation DLF/THM. In the Proof Control view, first disable the post-tactics (there is a small downward pointing arrow in the upper right hand corner above the toolbar (see Figure 2.22). Click on this arrow and make sure that the option Enable post-tactic is unchecked in the dropdown menu.) We are turning off the post-tactics because we want to see the proof develop in its different stages. Now select the root node in the Prove Tree, right-click on it and select Prune. This removes any proof that might be already started by the auto-provers. By doing this we want to assure that you have the same proof as in this tutorial.

Figure 2.22: Disabling the proof post-tactics in the Proof Controlling View

In order to succeed with the proof, we need a pair $p \mapsto l$ that is in *aut* but not in *sit*. Having a look the axioms, we find axm4 of doors_ctx1, which states that there is a location l different from *outside* where everyone is allowed to go:

 AXIOMS
   axm4 : $\exists l \cdot l \in L \setminus \{outside\} \wedge P \times \{l\} \subseteq aut$

So for every person p in P, $p \mapsto l$ and $p \mapsto outside$ are in *aut*. (In other words: every person is allowed to go to both the outside and a location l). The basic idea of our proof is that a person is either already outside or at the location l. If someone is outside, they are allowed to move to l, and if they are not outside, they are allowed to move outside. [12].

We assume that there is actually a person, so we need a set P that is non-empty. This is automatically the case since carrier sets are always non-empty, but we need a person as an example for our further proof. Now add the hypothesis $\exists x \cdot x \in P$ by entering this predicate into the Proof Control text area and hitting the ᵃʰ button. In the Proof Tree view you can now see three new nodes have appeared that need to be proven:

- $\top$ is the trivial well-definedness condition. Click on ♟ button to verify it.

- $\exists x \cdot x \in P$ is the hypothesis that we introduced. Click on the ♟ button to verify it.

- $\exists p, l \cdot (p \mapsto l \in aut \land sit(p) \neq l)$ is the original goal but we can now use the introduced hypothesis in the proof. We will now continue with the proof of this goal.

Click on the existential quantifier of the new hypothesis $\exists x \cdot x \in P$ (appearing in the Selected Hypothesis view) as demonstrated in Figure 2.23. The hypothesis disappears and is replaced by a new hypothesis $x \in P$. This is because the value of x is automatically instantiated. This means that we can use x from now on in our proof as an example for a person

 If you hover over any red symbol for a short while, a menu will pop up, offering one or more transformations. Make sure that you actually click on the symbol before the menu pops up because otherwise clicking will no longer have any effect. If the menu has popped up before you managed to click on the symbol, you will have to click twice: the first click will discard the menu and the next click will actually perform the operation.

We can prove an existential quantification by giving an example for the variables. First, we instantiate p in the goal with the variable x that we created: enter x in the yellow box corresponding to p in the Goal View and click on the existential quantifier as shown in Figure 2.24.

The instantiation produces two new nodes in the Proof Tree view. The first goal is the trivial well-definedness condition $\top$ and can be easily discharged by pressing ♟ . The remaining goal is $\exists l \cdot (x \mapsto l \in aut \land sit(x) \neq l)$ is the result of replacing p by x in the old goal. You can see the the current proof tree in Figure 2.25. The node with the label ah refers to when we added the hypothesis, the node with the label $\exists$ hyp refers to when we instantiated x from a hypothesis and the node with the label $\exists$ goal refers to when we instantiated p in the goal.

---

[12]One could argue that this is too restrictive in the real world: After all, why do all people need authorisation for the *same* location l? But arguing about the realism of the example is out of the scope.

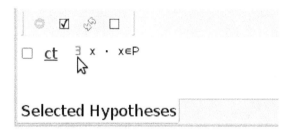

Figure 2.23: Click on the existential quantifier in order to ...

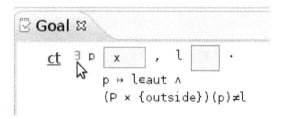

Figure 2.24: ... instantiate it, in this case by substituting x.

Figure 2.25: The proof tree after instantiating p with x.

Now we need an example for the remaining variable l. There are two situations we want to distinguish: The person x could be outside or not. To distinguish this, type $sit(x) = outside$ into the Proof Control view and click on the button ^{dc} (dc for distinguish case). Again, you get three new goals.

- The first is the well-definedness condition of $sit(x) = outside$. sit must be a function and x is in its domain. This is easy to prove since sit is a total function (3.3.5). Press the button to verify it.

- The second node has the original goal but $sit(x) = outside$ as a hypothesis.

- The third node has the original goal but $\neg sit(x) = outside$ as a hypothesis.

Note that the second and third node will appear identical in the
proof tree. You will only see the differences in the hypotheses by
selecting the nodes.

Let's continue with the case $sit(x) = outside$: When x is outside, it can
always go to the l that is defined axm4. To search for axm4, type $outside$
into the Proof Control text field and click the button ⬚ . Add axm4 ($\exists l \cdot l \in$
$L \setminus \{outside\} \wedge P \times \{l\} \subseteq aut$) to the selected hypotheses. Now click on the
red $\exists$ symbol in axm4 (see Figure 2.26) to instantiate l. Now we have l as an
example for a location which is not outside and where everybody can go. Our

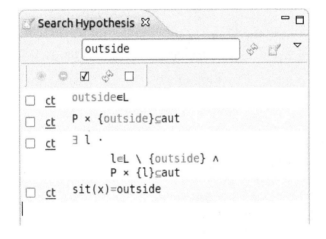

Figure 2.26: Searching hypothesis for $outside$: The third one is axm4.

goal is still $\exists l \cdot x \mapsto l \in aut \wedge sit(x) \neq l$. Note that the existential quantification
introduces a new l which does not (yet) have anything to do with the location
l where anybody can go. Now type l into the yellow box of the goal and press
the $\exists$ symbol to state that we want to use our l as an example for the l in the
existential quantification. Again, we have the trivial goal $\top$ as well-definedness
condition, so just press ⚓ button to verify it. The remaining goal should be
$x \mapsto l \in aut \wedge sit(x) \neq l$. This can be proven with the selected hypotheses
$sit(x) = outside$, $l \in L \setminus \{outside\}$ and $P \times \{l\} \subseteq aut$. Press the ⚓ button to
verify this goal.

Now only second case of the case distinction remains. This is where x is
not outside ($sit(x) \neq outside$). In this case, x can simply go outside. Again
the goal is $\exists l \cdot x \mapsto l \in aut \wedge sit(x) \neq l$. Type $outside$ as an example for a
location l into the yellow box and press the $\exists$ symbol. Press the ⚓ button

to discharge the trivial well-definedness condition ⊤. The new goal should be $x \mapsto outside \in aut \wedge sit(x) \neq outside$.

To prove this we need to prove that x has the right to go *outside*. This is stated in the axiom $P \times \{outside\} \subseteq aut$. Have a look at the Search Hypothesis view. This was also one of the results from the last search for *outside*. (If you no longer see the results, repeat the search by entering *outside* into the Proof Control and press the ✐ button.) Select $P \times \{outside\} \subseteq aut$ (in Figure 2.26, it's the second entry) and press the ✱ button to add it to your selected hypothesis. The auto-prover now has enough hypotheses, so simply click the ⚕ button and the last goal of our theorem should be proven.

Here is the summary of the proof. Compare this with your final proof tree (as shown in Figure 2.27).

---

added hypotheses: $\exists x \cdot x \in P$
    well-definedness condition ⊤: automatically proven
    the hypotheses: automatically proven
    instantiation of x in the hypotheses $\exists x \cdot x \in P$
        using x as an example for the $\exists p \ldots$ in the goal
            well-definedness condition ⊤: automatically proven
            case distinction $sit(x) = outside$
                well-definedness condition (*sit* is a function with x in its
                              domain): proven using the p1 provers
             first case: instantiation of l from axiom axm4
                using l as an example for the $\exists l \ldots$ in the goal
                    well-definedness condition ⊤: automatically proven
                    remaining goal: automatically proven
             second case: using *outside* as an example
                        for the $\exists l \ldots$ in the goal
                well-definedness condition ⊤: automatically proven
                hypotheses $P \times \{outside\}$ selected
                remaining goal: automatically proven

2.10.2   Deadlock Freeness of First Refinement

Now we are going to explain the main complexity of our model: the deadlock freeness proof for the first refinement.

 Please remember that post-tactics should still be disabled before starting this part of the tutorial.

The difference between the first refinement and the initial model is that a new constant com has been added in order to describe which rooms are connected. Additionally, we have a constant exit, which allows anybody to get outside. Please consult the Event-B book (1.2.1) for the details regarding this model.

The event INITIALISATION does not change, but the event PASS is refined as a consequence. We assume that a person can move to another location l if they have the authorisation to be in l (already defined in the abstraction) and

Figure 2.27: Searching hypothesis for *outside*: The third one is axm4.

also if the location l is connected to the location p where the person is at this
precise moment (represented by $sit(p)$).

grd12 : $sit(p) \mapsto l \in com$

As in the last section (2.10.1), open the door_1 machine and add a derived
invariant (theorem) called DLF as follows[13]:

DLF : $\exists q, m \cdot (q \mapsto m \in aut \wedge sit(q) \mapsto m \in com)$

Save the file. Once again, the prover fails to prove this theorem automatically. What we want to prove is that "at least one person authorized to be in a
location must also be authorized to go in another location which communicates
with the first one".

---

[13]In the future, it might be worthwhile to change this theorem to take care of a couple of
issues. It only states that at least one person can move, and it may be better to state that
every person can move. Furthermore, this statement is unable to detect live locks: A situation
where the system oscillates between a small number of states.

Switch over to the proving perspective and double click on DLF/THM to begin proving. When getting started, it is often a good idea to subdivide a proof into cases. In this case, one distinction of cases should be to determine whether the person is outside or not.

First we need a variable denoting a location in order to distinguish between the two cases. We use the deadlock freeness invariant from the initial model for this purpose. Search through the possible hypotheses and add this theorem to the selected hypotheses (Figure 2.28).

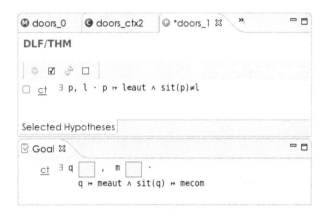

Figure 2.28: Adding a hypothesis to instantiate a variable for a case distinction.

Now click on the red ∃ to instantiate the variables p and l. This will allow us to make the case distinction. To do this, we enter the following in the Proof Control View:

$$sit(p) = outside$$

Now press the ᵈᵉ button. This will create three new nodes in the proof tree: The first one is once again the well-definedness condition, followed by the two cases that we have just defined. As always, use the ♟ button to verify the well-definedness condition.

The first case is dealing with $sit(p) = outside$. To verify this case, we need to use axm7, which states that at least one authorized room is connected to the outside:

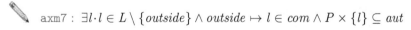
axm7 : $∃l·l ∈ L \setminus \{outside\} ∧ outside \mapsto l ∈ com ∧ P × \{l\} ⊆ aut$

Add axm7 to the list of hypotheses. We would like to work with an instance of a location, so we instantiate this hypothesis by clicking on its red ∃ symbol.

ℹ️ Note that Rodin instantiated the variable with the name $l0$ instead of l because the name l already exists from the previous instantiation.

Now we have variables to instantiate our goal as well. We enter the value p in the yellow box for q and $l0$ in the yellow box for m (see Figure 2.29) and press the red $\exists$.

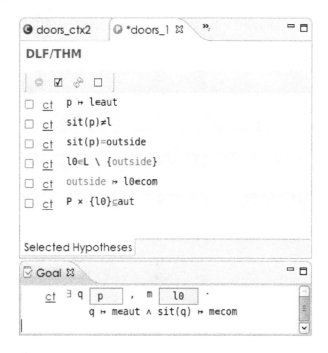

Figure 2.29: Preparing the instantiation by providing values for p and $l0$.

This results in two new nodes to the proof tree, the first one being the well-defined proof obligation. The last remaining proof obligation can be solved with the given hypotheses. Clicking will discharge both of these proof obligations.

Now the first case is resolved. Now let's consider the second case, $sit(p) \neq outside$. We would like to instantiate the quantifier again, but this time we have to use different values. We still have p to substitute for q, but for the location we use the exit relationship: Our axioms tell us that there is always an exit from every location, so $exit(sit(p))$ should be a valid substitution for m. Let's perform the substitution. This advances our proof tree with a new node (and the well-definedness proof obligation, which we discharge with one click).

The resulting proof obligation is a conjunction. We can discharge the two parts of it by clicking on the red $\wedge$ symbol in the goal view. This results in two simpler goals in the proof tree. We start with the **second** goal.

> We start with the second goal instead of the first goal because doing so will provide us with hypotheses that will be beneficial in discharging the first goal. How do we know this? By experience and by playing with the proofs for a long time. Depressingly, there is no

easy rule to guide us through the proving process. There are just general guidelines and experience.

The goal we start with is:

$$sit(p) \mapsto exit(sit(p)) \in com$$

None the hypotheses that we have added so far contain *com*, so add axm4 to the selected hypotheses:

axm4 : $exit \subseteq com$

Hit the $_{p0}$ button, and Rodin discharges the goal.
Now deal with the last undischarged goal:

$$p \mapsto exit(sit(p)) \in aut$$

This statement means that the person is authorized to follow the exit. To discharge this proof obligation we need to use axm6, which essentially states that "Everybody has the permission to leave from wherever they are":

axm6 : $aut \rhd \{outside\} \subseteq (aut; exit^{-1})$

Remove the inclusion by clicking on the red $\subseteq$, which results in a hypothesis with universal quantifier. Instantiate this with the variables that we already have on hand. Instantiate x with p and x0 with sit(p). Examine this formula and try to understand what it means.

This results in two more goals in our proof tree. The first goal is the well-definedness condition which we discharge with the 🏆 button.

The remaining goal is simple and essentially states that following the current position along the exit route will lead to a location where the user is authorized:

$$p \subseteq exit(sit(p)) \in aut$$

We cannot discharge this with the $_{p0}$ prover; However, using the $_{p1}$ prover will discharge it. Using $_{p1}$ is the same as selecting related hypotheses with 🔍 and then using $_{p0}$. The danger of this approach is that if too many hypotheses are added, the prover may not be able to find a solution before timing out. In this case, it worked.

As an exercise, try to manually identify the hypotheses that were required to discharge this goal.

This concludes this section of the tutorial. Be aware that we have just looked at one small aspect of a rather sophisticated model. Also, please be aware that this tutorial gave you only an introduction to proving. To become an expert, we encourage you to study interesting models and to practice.

2.11   Outlook

Congratulations – if you have made it this far, you should have a good foundation for getting some real work done with Rodin. In this section we would like to provide you with a few pointers that will help you to make your work as efficient as possible.

Use the Reference Section and FAQ If you have a specific issue or if you quickly need to look something up, check the reference (3) and FAQ (4) of this handbook.

Online, PDF and Eclipse-Version of the Handbook There are three versions of this handbook. You can access it directly through Rodin by using the built-in help browser (Help ⟩ Help Contents). The Eclipse-Version is useful because it can be used offline.

Use the Rodin Wiki The Rodin Wiki (1.1.2) contains the latest news regarding Rodin and a wealth of information that is not in the scope of this handbook. Be sure to check out it out.

Find useful Plugins There are many plugins available, so be sure to check them out. There is a good chance that they will make your life easier.

Subscribe to the mailing lists The wiki lists the existing mailing lists (4.1.1) which include a list for users and for developers. We strongly recommend subscribing to the announcement list.

Rodin in Industry If you are considering using Rodin in an industrial setting, be sure to explore the testimonies from the Deploy (1.5) project, in which industrial partners describe their experiences with Rodin.

We wish you success in your modelling projects!

Chapter 3

Reference

3.1 The Rodin Platform

In this section, we describe the details of the tool platform, as it is presented to the user. You will find a description of all GUI elements that you may encounter.

3.1.1 Eclipse in General

From the Eclipse Website[1]**:** Eclipse is an open source community, whose projects are focused on building an open development platform comprised of extensible frameworks, tools and runtimes for building, deploying and managing software across the lifecycle. The Eclipse Foundation is a not-for-profit, member supported corporation that hosts the Eclipse projects and helps cultivate both an open source community and an ecosystem of complementary products and services.

From Wikipedia[2]**:** Eclipse is a multi-language software development environment comprising an integrated development environment (IDE) and an extensible plugin system. It is written mostly in Java and can be used to develop applications in Java and, by means of various plugins, other programming languages including Ada, C, C++, COBOL, Perl, PHP, Python, R, Ruby (including Ruby on Rails framework), Scala, Clojure, Groovy and Scheme. It can also be used to develop packages for the software Mathematica. The IDE is often called Eclipse ADT (Ada Development Toolkit) for Ada, Eclipse CDT for C/C++, Eclipse JDT for Java, and Eclipse PDT for PHP.

Eclipse provides the technical foundation of Rodin.

---

[1]http://www.eclipse.org/
[2]http://en.wikipedia.org/

Project Constituents and Relationships

The primary concept in doing formal developments with the Rodin Platform is that of a project. A project contains the complete mathematical development of a Discrete Transition System. It consists of components of two different types: machines and contexts. Machines contain the variables, invariants, theorems, and events for a project. Contexts contain the carrier sets, constants, axioms, and theorems for a project. Figure 3.1 shows an overview.

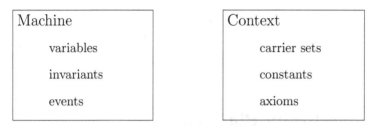

Figure 3.1: Overview Machine and Context

Various relationships exist between machines and contexts. This is illustrated in the following figure. A machine can be "refined" by another one, and a context can be "extended" by another one. However, cycles are not allowed (i.e. the original machine cannot refine any of the refined machines). A machine can also "see" one or several contexts. A typical example of machine and context relationship is shown in Figure 3.2.

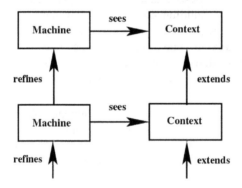

Figure 3.2: A typical example of machine and context relationship

Rodin Nature

Eclipse Projects can have one or more natures to describe their purpose. The GUI then adapt to this nature. Rodin Projects must have the Rodin-Nature. If you create an Event-B project in Rodin, it automatically has the right nature.

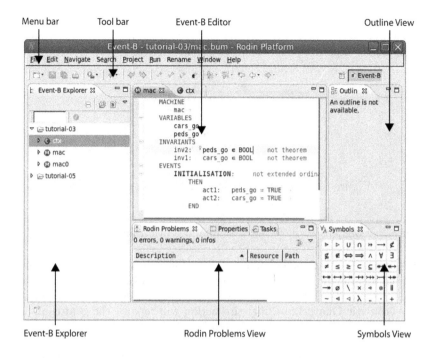

Figure 3.3: Overview of the Event-B Perspective

If you want to modify an existing project, you can edit the `.project` file and add the following XML in the `<natures>` section:

   `<nature>org.rodinp.core.rodinnature</nature>`

3.1.2 The Event-B Perspective

Figure 3.3 shows an overview of the opening window of the Event-B Perspective. The following subsections identify the different Rodin GUI elements (i.e. views) which are visible and explain their functions.

Menu bar

The menu bar provides file and edit operations and other useful Event-B specific operations. We will briefly describe the most important menu items here.

Rename menu   When opening a machine or context file, the following actions for automatically renaming the Event-B model elements are available for the user:

One action is available when editing context files (see Figure 3.4).

- Automatic Axiom Labelling: this action will rename the axioms alphanumerically according to their order of appearance.

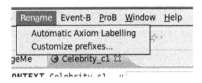

Figure 3.4: Automatic rename actions for context files

Three actions are available for machine files (see Figure 3.5).

- Automatic Invariant Labelling: this action will rename the invariants alphanumerically according to their order of appearance.

- Automatic Guard Labelling: this action will rename the guards alphanumerically according to their order of appearance,

- Automatic Action Labelling: this action will rename the actions alphanumerically according to their order of appearance.

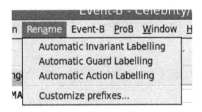

Figure 3.5: Automatic rename actions for machine files

Event-B menu   When opening a machine or context file, some wizards for creating Event-B model elements are available for the user. The different wizards are described in Section 3.1.6.

Tool bar

The tool bar provides shortcuts for familiar commands like save, print, undo and redo. The tool bar also provides shortcuts to the wizards for creating elements like axioms, constants, enumerated sets, etc., which are described in Section 3.1.6.

Editor View

The editor view contains the active Event-B editor which is described in Section 3.1.4.

Outline View

The outline view displays the outline of the active Event-B editor and lists elements like axioms, variables, etc..

Rodin Problems View

When an error is discovered in a project, a ⊗ marker appears next to the line with the problem in the editor view, and the faulty component in the Event-B Explorer is also similarly marked with ▨ . The error itself (e.g. a syntax error) is shown in the Rodin Problems view.

By double-clicking on the error statement, you are transferred automatically to the place where the error has been detected so that you can correct it easily.

Symbols View

The symbols view is intended to give users a convenient way to add mathematical symbols to the various model editors. If an editor is open and a text field is active (the cursor is blinking), clicking a symbol will insert it at the current position (see Figure 3.6).

The ASCII code corresponding to the symbol over which the mouse hovers is also displayed as a tooltip so that the user can also learn how to input symbols directly.

Event-B Explorer

Projects can be found in the RODIN platform in the Event-B Explorer. This is usually situated on the left hand side of the screen as shown in Figure 3.3. The Event-B Explorer contains a list of name of the current projects. Next to each project name is a ▷ button. By pressing it, one can expand a project and see the machines and contexts that it contains.

The icons (⊙ or Ⓜ) next to the component name identifies whether it is a context or machine respectively.

When expanding a machine or a context, you can explore its elements. Double clicking on a specific element (i.e. a variable) opens the Event-B editor and marks the position of the variable in the machine or context as shown in Figure 3.7. Furthermore, proof obligations are displayed when clicking on the small triangle next to the label Proof Obligations (for more information see Section 3.1.7).

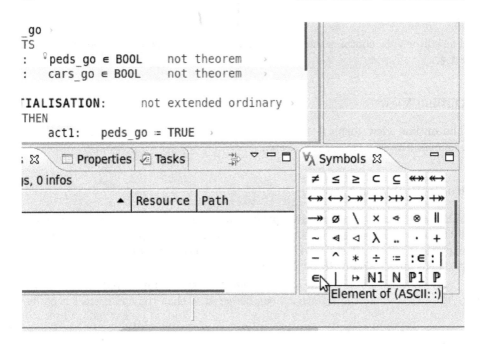

Figure 3.6: Clicking a symbol inserts it at the current position

3.1.3   Customizing a perspective suitable for RODIN

So far, you have needed two different perspectives to work with RODIN. However, it is actually possible to work with only one perspective. In this section,
we will try to customize a perspective so that we do not need any other. If you
have experience with customizing Eclipse perspectives, you may only want to
read the next paragraph which contains a few suggestions for a good perspective
for RODIN.

We should start by thinking about how we want our perspective to appear.
The proving perspective already is quite nice, but we may want to use a little
bit more editing space when in the Event-B perspective. To create more space,
we can move all windows that currently are on both sides of the editing area
onto one side since they never really need to be used simultaneously. We can
also dock all of these windows onto the so-called Fast View bar so that they
disappear when they are not needed. It would also be nice to be able to split
the screen and work on several components at once. Then we could edit both
the abstract machine and the concrete machine at the same time.

For the most part, the perspectives can be customized by dragging and
dropping the different windows. First of all, you need to find the Fast View
bar. Usually, it is at the bottom of the Eclipse window, but it also can be on
the side or hidden inside the Shortcut Bar. For our purposes, it probably is
best to have it on the right side of the screen. Place it there by dragging and

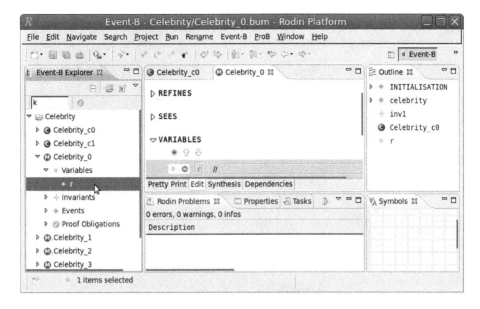

Figure 3.7: Double clicking on an element opens the Event-B editor and marks the corresponding position

dropping it with the mouse. Now add some items to it. To do this, press the Show View as a Fast View button on the bar (See Figure 3.8). It may be a good idea to to leave the Goal, the Rodin Problems and the Proof Control views open at the bottom of the screen since you may want them to stay open while editing. A good selection of views to add to the Fast View bar may be:

- Project Explorer

- Search Hypothesis

- Cache Hypothesis

- Proof Tree

- Proof Information

- Progress Window

All of the windows that you cannot create directly when clicking on Show View as a Fast View can be found under Others/General. After you are finished, the window should look like Figure 3.9. Click on "Save Perspective As..." in the Window menu to save the perspective.

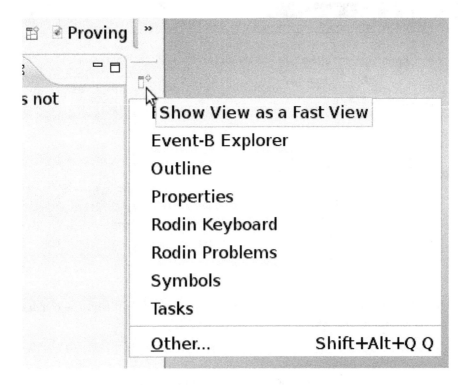

Figure 3.8: Show View as a Fast View

3.1.4   The Event-B Editor

Once a context or a machine is created, a window appears in the editing area
as shown in Figure 3.10.

 The editor described here was made the default editor in Rodin 2.4
(February 2012) and still has some minor issues (see Section 4.3.12).
The alternative structural editor is still available (see Section 3.1.5).

The editor allows you to edit the modelling elements of the context which
are the dependencies, the carrier sets, the constants, and the axioms. By right-
clicking in predefined places you can create new modelling elements. For instance, a ⸴ symbol appears directly to the right of the name of the context
(in this case, the name of the context is "ctx"). Place your cursor directly to
the left of this symbol and right click. Select the element that you would like
to add from the Add Child menu as shown in Figure 3.11.

Machine elements can also be added in the same way.

To remove a modelling element, right click on the modelling element and
select Delete.

It is also possible to add modelling elements by using wizards (See 3.1.6).

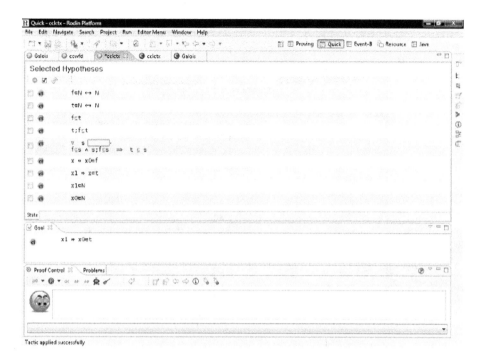

Figure 3.9: Our self-made Quick perspective

Figure 3.10: The Event-B editor

3.1.5 The Structural Event-B Editor

The editor described here was the default editor until Rodin 2.3. It is still available. To use this editor, right click on a machine or context file in the Event-B Explorer and select Open With ⟩ Event-B

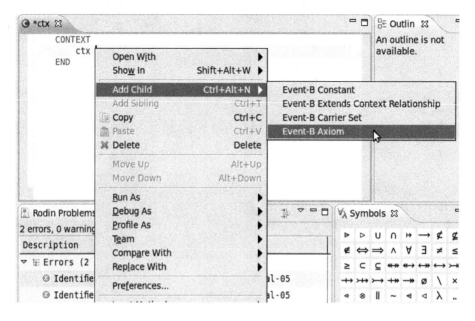

Figure 3.11: Adding a new modelling element

Machine Editor.

Once a context or a machine is created, a window appears in the editing area as shown in Figure 3.12.

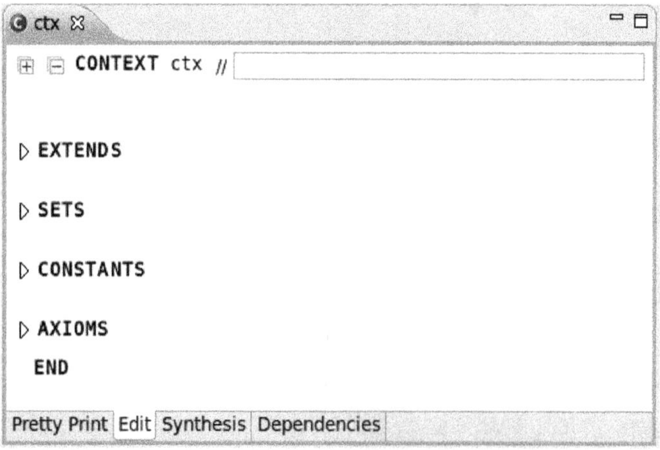

Figure 3.12: The Structured Event-B editor

By default, you are in Edit mode which allows you to edit the modelling elements of the context (the dependencies, the carrier sets, the constants, and the axioms). By right-clicking on the modelling elements you can create new child and sibling elements. For instance, by pressing the triangle (▷) next to each keyword, you can see the different modelling elements and also add, remove, or move them. Figure 3.13 shows what the section looks like after pressing the triangle next to the keyword "AXIOMS".

Figure 3.13: By pressing the triangle you can collapse/expand context sections

By pressing the ✳ button, you can add a new modelling element. For instance, clicking on the ✳ button in the AXIOMS section will add a new axiom element. You can now enter a new axiom and a comment in the corresponding boxes as indicated in Figure 3.14.

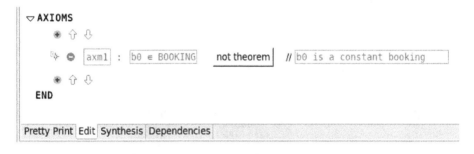

Figure 3.14: Adding a new modelling element

To remove a modelling element, press the ⊖ button. You can also move an modelling element up or down by selecting it and then pressing one of the two arrows (⇧ or ⇩).

Dependencies (Context)

By selecting the Dependencies tab at the bottom of the Event-B editor, you obtain the window shown in Figure 3.15.

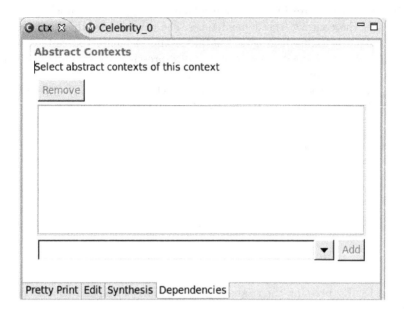

Figure 3.15: Dependencies tab of the Event-B editor

The dependencies tab allows you to control the other contexts that the current context extends. To add the context that you want to extend, select the name of the context from the drop-down menu at the bottom of the window and then hit the **Add** button.

There is also another way to create a new context as an extension existing one. Select the context in the project window and then press the right mouse key. Then select **Extend** from the menu that opens up. This should bring up the window as shown in Figure 3.16.

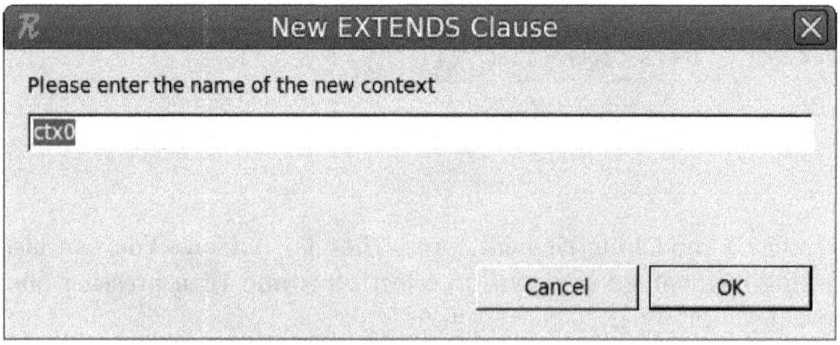

Figure 3.16: New EXTENDS Clause window

You can then enter the name of the new context which will automatically extend your chosen context.

Dependencies (Machine)

The Dependencies tab for machines is very similar to the one for contexts that is described in the previous section. The main difference is that there are two kinds of dependencies that can be established: machines on which the current machine depends are listed in the upper part and contexts on which the current machine depends are listed in the lower part.

Synthesis (Context)

Selecting the Synthesis tab brings up a global view of your context's elements (carrier set / constant / axiom / extended context) as demonstrated in Figure 3.17.

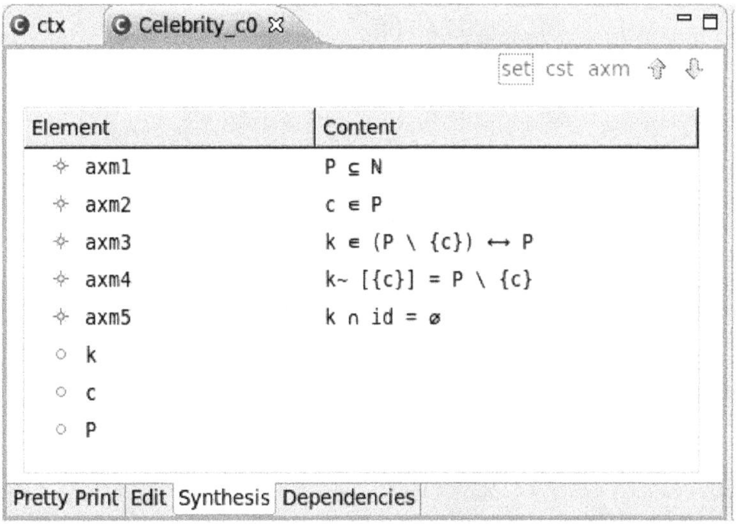

Figure 3.17: The Synthesis tab of the Event-B editor

By pressing the set, cst, or axm buttons in the upper right corner, you can filter out the carrier sets, constants or axioms of your context respectively.

If you select an element, you can change its priority by pressing the ⇧ button or the ⇩ button. You do this for axioms, carrier sets, constants and extended contexts.

Right clicking in this view will bring up a context menu that allows you to add a new carrier set, constant, axiom or extended context.

Synthesis (Machine)

The Synthesis tab for machines is very similar to the one of contexts (see above) except that you have a global view of your machine's elements (refined machines, seen contexts, variables, invariants, events, and variants).

Pretty Print

Selecting the Pretty Print tab gives you a global view of your context or machine as if it had been entered through with an input text file as seen in Figure 3.18.

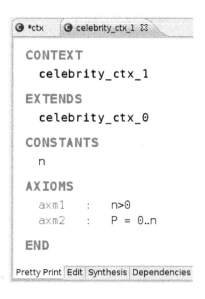

Figure 3.18: The Pretty Print tab of the Event-B editor

3.1.6 Wizards

In addition to being able to directly enter modelling elements in the editor, it is also possible to add them by using wizards. You can activate the different wizards by using the buttons in the tool bar as shown in Figure 3.19 and in Figure 3.20 or via the Event-B menu (the menu will only provide the wizards that you need for creating your machine components or context components). The next sections explain how to use the wizards.

Figure 3.19: Wizards for context specific elements located in the tool bar

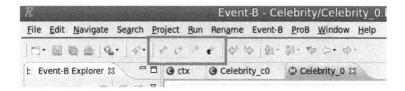

Figure 3.20: Wizards for machine specific elements located in the tool bar

New Carrier Sets Wizard

To activate the New Carrier Sets Wizard, press the s^+ button located in the tool bar. Pressing the button bring up the window shown in Figure 3.21.

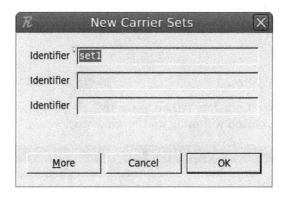

Figure 3.21: New Carrier Sets Wizard

You can enter as many carrier sets as you want by pressing the More button. When you are finished, press the OK button.

New Enumerated Set Wizard

To activate the New Enumerated Set Wizard, press the s^+ button located in the tool bar. Pressing the button bring up the window shown in Figure 3.22.

Enter the name of the new enumerated set as well as the names of its elements. By pressing the More Elements button, you can enter additional elements. When you're finished, press the OK button. The benefit of using this wizard is that in addition to creating the set and its elements, the wizard automatically creates the axiom that is necessary for the context to work. For example, when you add the new carrier set COLOUR and the three constants red, green, and orange, the wizard automatically creates the following axiom

$$partition(COLOUR, \{red\}, \{green\}, \{orange\})$$

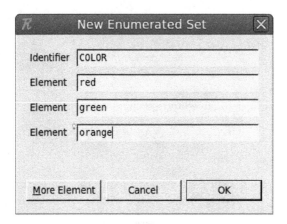

Figure 3.22: New Enumerated Set Wizard

New Constants Wizard

To activate the New Constants Wizard, press the $c^\diamond$ button located in the tool bar. Pressing the button will bring up the window shown in Figure 3.23.

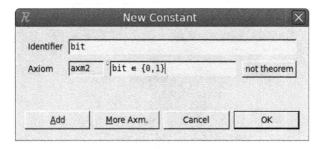

Figure 3.23: New Constants Wizard

You can then enter the names of a constant and an axiom which can be used to define the constant's type. By pressing the More Axm. button you can enter additional axioms. To add more constants, press the Add button. When you have finished, press the OK button.

New Axioms Wizard

To activate the New Axioms Wizard, press the $\alpha^\diamond$ button located in the tool bar. Pressing the button brings up the window shown in Figure 3.24.

You can then enter the axioms you want. If more axioms are needed, press the More button. When you are finished, press the OK button.

Check the "Theorem" checkbox if the corresponding axiom that you created should be marked as a a a theorem.

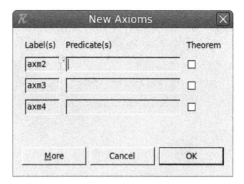

Figure 3.24: New Axioms Wizard

New Variable Wizard

To activate the New Variable Wizard, press the 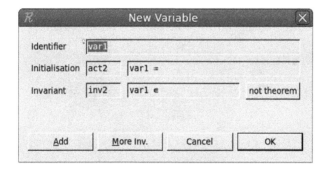 button located in the tool bar. Pressing the button brings up the window shown in Figure 3.25.

Figure 3.25: New Variable Wizard

You can then enter the names of the variable, what its state at initialisation should be, and an invariant which defines its type. By pressing button More Inv., you can enter additional invariants. To add more variables, press the Add button. When you're finished, press the OK button.

New Invariants Wizard

To activate the New Invariants Wizard, press the ι^+ button located in the tool bar. Pressing the button bring up the window shown in Figure 3.26.

You can then enter the invariants you want. If more invariants are needed, press the More button. Check the Theorem checkbox to indicate that the corresponding invariant should be marked as a theorem.

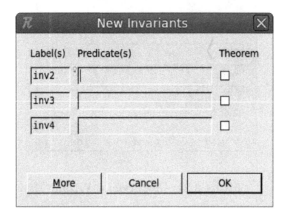

Figure 3.26: New Invariants Wizard

New Event Wizard

To activate the New Events Wizard, press the ✎ button located in the tool bar. Pressing this button brings up the window shown in Figure 3.27.

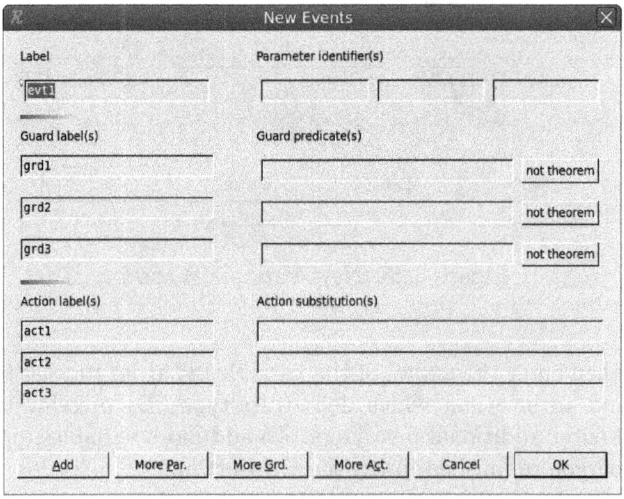

Figure 3.27: New Event Wizard

You can then enter the events that you want. As indicated, the following elements can be entered: name, parameters, guards, and actions. More parameters, guards and actions can be entered by pressing the corresponding buttons. If more events are needed, press the Add button. Press the OK button when you're finished.

Menu bar   Tool bar   Name of PO   Selected Hyptotheses   Event-B Explorer

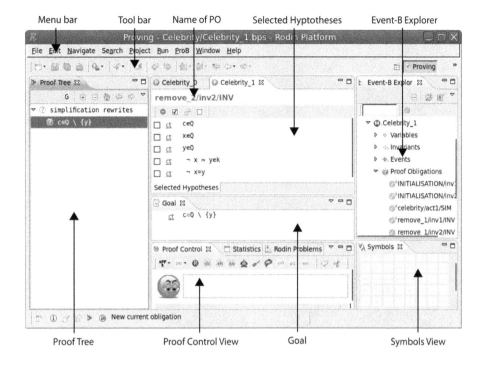

Proof Tree   Proof Control View   Goal   Symbols View

Figure 3.28: Overview of the Proving Perspective

Note that an event with no guard is considered to the guard *true*. Also, an event with no action is considered to have the action *skip*.

3.1.7   The Proving Perspective

When proof obligations (POs) (3.2.7) are not discharged automatically, the user can attempt to discharge them interactively using the Proving Perspective. This page provides an overview of the Proving Perspective and its use. If the Proving Perspective is not visible as a tab on the top right-hand corner of the main interface, the user can switch to it via Window ⟩ Open Perspective.

The Proving Perspective consists of a number of views: the Proof Tree, the Goal, the Selected Hypotheses, the Proof Control, the Search Hypotheses, the Cache Hypotheses and the Proof Information. In the discussion that follows we look at each of these views individually. Figure 3.28 shows an overview of the Proving Perspective.

Loading a Proof

To work on an PO that has not yet been discharged, it is necessary to load the proof into the Proving Perspective. To do this, switch to the Proving Perspective. Select the project from the Event-B Explorer and select and expand the component (context or machine). Finally, select (double-click) the proof obligation of interest. A number of views will be updated with details of the corresponding proof.

Note that pressing the ⊘ button on the top left hand side of the Event-B Explorer will remove all discharged proof obligations (POs) from the view.

The Proof Tree

The proof tree view provides a graphical representation of each individual proof step as seen in Figure 3.29.

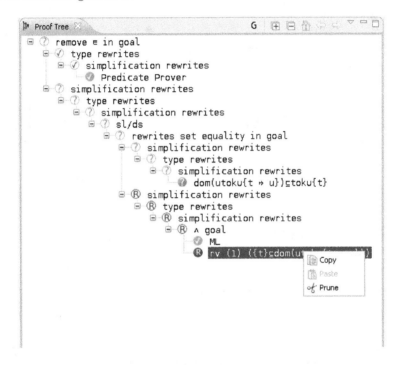

Figure 3.29: The Proof Tree

The tree is made up of sequents. A line of the tree is shifted to the right when the corresponding node is a direct descendant of the node of the previous line. Each sequent is labeled with a comment which indicates which rule has been applied or which prover discharged the proof. By selecting a sequent in the proof tree, the hypotheses of the sequent are loaded to the Selected Hypotheses window, and the goal of the sequent is loaded to the Goal view.

Decoration   The symbol to the left of the leaf indicates the state of the sequent:

- ⬗ indicates that this sequent is discharged.

- ⬗ indicates that this sequent is not discharged.

- Ⓡ indicates that this sequent has been reviewed.

Internal nodes in the proof display the symbols with the colours inverted. Note that a "reviewed" sequent is one that is not yet discharged by the prover. Instead, it has been "seen" by the user who decided to postpone the proof. Marking sequents as "reviewed" is very convenient since the provers will ignore these leaves and focus on specific areas of interest. This allows the proof to be discharged interactively in a gradual fashion. In order to discharge a "reviewed" sequent, select it and prune the tree at that node: the node will become "brown" again (undischarged), and you can now try to discharge it.

Navigation within the Proof Tree There are three buttons on the top of the proof tree view:

- G allows you to see the goal of corresponding to each node.

- ⊞ allows you to fully expand the proof tree.

- ⊟ allows you to fully collapse the tree; only the root stays visible.

Manipulating the Proof Tree

Hiding The button next to each node in the proof tree allows you to expand or collapse the subtree starting at that node.

Pruning The proof tree can be pruned at a selected node. This means that the subtree of the selected node is removed from the proof tree. The selected node becomes a leaf and displays the symbol ⬗ . The proof activity can then be resumed from this node. After selecting a node in the proof tree, pruning can be performed in two ways:

- by right-clicking and selecting Prune,

- by clicking on the ⚲ button in the proof control view.

Note that after pruning, the post-tactic is not applied to the new current sequent. The post-tactic should be applied manually, if required, by clicking on the post-tactic button in the Proof Control view. This is especially useful when you want to redo a proof from the beginning. The proof tree can be pruned at its root node and then the proof can proceed again with invocation of internal or external provers or with an interactive proof.

Before pruning a particular node, the node (and its subtree) can be copied to the clipboard. If the new proof strategy subsequently fails, the copied version can be pasted back into the pruned node (explained further in the next section).

Copy/Paste By selecting a node in the proof tree and then right-clicking with the mouse, you can copy the part of the proof tree starting at that sequent (including the node and its subtree). Pasting the node and subtree back in is done in a similar manner with a right mouse click on a proof node. This allows you to reuse a part of a proof tree in the same proof or even in another proof.

Goal and Selected Hypotheses

Each sequent in the proof tree have corresponding hypotheses and goals. A user will work with one selected sequent at a time by attempting various strategies in an effort to show that the goal is true. The Goal and Selected Hypotheses views provide information to the user about the currently selected sequent. Figure 3.30 shows an example.

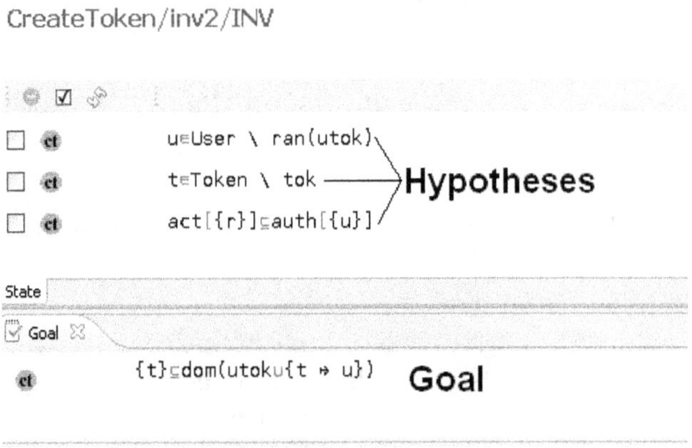

Figure 3.30: Open proof obligation

A hypothesis can be removed from the list of selected hypotheses by selecting the check the box situated next to it (you can click on several boxes at once) and then by clicking on the ⊖ button at the top of the selected hypotheses window.

Note that the deselected hypotheses are not lost. You can find them again using the Search Hypotheses ⊡ button in the Proof Control view. Other buttons are used as follows:

- ☑ - Select all hypotheses.

- ⌀ - Invert the selection.

- ⊄ next to the goal - Proof by contradiction 1: The negation of the goal becomes a selected hypothesis and the goal becomes "⊥".

- ⊄ next to a selected hypothesis - Proof by contradiction 2: The negation of the hypothesis becomes the goal and the negated goal becomes a selected hypothesis.

A user wishing to attempt an interactive proof has a number of proof rules available, and these may either rewrite a hypothesis/goal or infer something from it. In the Goal and the Selected Hypotheses views, various operators may appear in red coloured font. The red font indicates that some interactive proof rule(s) are applicable and may be applied as a step in the proof attempt. When the mouse hovers over such an operator, a number of applicable rules may be displayed; the user may choose to apply one of the rules by clicking on it. Figure 3.31 shows an example.

Other proof rules can be applied when green buttons appear in the Goal and Selected Hypotheses views. Examples are proof by contradiction ⬚ and conjunction introduction ∧ .

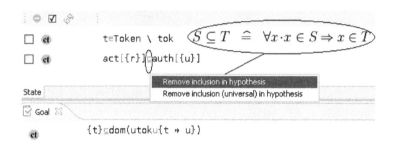

Figure 3.31: Applying a rule

To instantiate a quantifier, the user enters the desired expression in the yellow box behind the quantifier and clicks on the quantifier (the red ∃) as demonstrated in Figure 3.32.

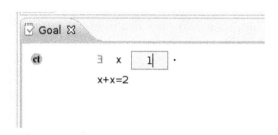

Figure 3.32: Instantiating a quantifier

The Proof Control View

The Proof Control view contains the buttons with which you can perform an interactive proof. An overview of this proof can be seen in Figure 3.33.

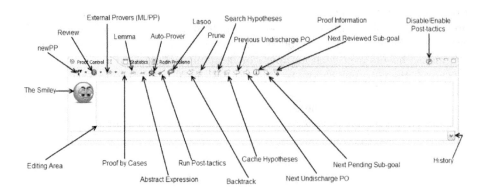

Figure 3.33: The Proof Control View

The following buttons are available in the Proof Control view:

- ᴾᴾ invokes the new predicate prover. A drop-down list indicates alternative strategies.

- ⓡ indicates that a node has been reviewed. In an attempt by the user to carry out sequents in a certain order, they might decide to postpone the task of discharging some sequents until a later stage. To do this, the sequent can be marked as reviewed by choosing the correct node and clicking on this button. This indicates that by visually checking the sequent, the user is convinced that they can discharge it later, but they do not want to do it right now.

- ᵖᵒ external provers can be invoked from the drop-down list to test sequents.

- ᵈᶜ begins a proof by cases. The proof is split into two branches. In the first branch, the predicate supplied by the user is added to the Selected Hypotheses, and the user attempts to discharge this branch. In the second branch, the predicate supplied by the user is negated and added to the Selected Hypotheses. The user then attempts to discharge this branch.

- ᵃʰ adds a new hypothesis. The predicate in the editing area should be proved by the user. It is then added as a new selected hypothesis.

- ᵃᵉ adds an abstract expression. The expression in the editing area is given a fresh name.

- ♟ invokes the auto prover which attempts to discharge the goal. The auto-prover is applied automatically on all proof obligations after a the machine or context is saved. Using this button, you can invoke the auto-prover within an interactive proof.

- ✔ executes the post-tactics.

- ☙ loads the hidden hypotheses that contain identifiers in common with the goal and with the selected hypotheses into the Selected Hypotheses window

- ♡ backtracks from the current node (i.e., prunes its parent).

- ✂ prunes the proof tree from the node selected in the proof tree.

- ☞ finds hypotheses containing the character string in the editing area and displays them in the Search Hypothesis view.

- ☟ displays the Cache Hypotheses view. This view displays all hypotheses that are related to the current goal.

- ⇦ loads the preceding undischarged proof obligation.

- ⇨ loads the next undischarged proof obligation,

- ① displays information regarding the current proof obligation in the corresponding window. This information corresponds to the elements that directly took part in the generation of the proof obligation (events, invariant, etc.).

- ☙ moves to the next pending node of the current proof tree,

- ☙ loads the next reviewed node of the current proof tree.

You can also disable/enable post-tactics which allows you to decide if post-tactics should run after each interactive proof step. In addition, you can open the preferences for post-tactics. To do this, open the menu of the Proof Control view via the ▽ button in the upper right corner of the view.

The Smiley The smiley can be one of three different colours:

1. red indicates that the proof tree contains one or more undischarged sequents

2. blue indicates that all undischarged sequents of the proof tree have been reviewed

3. green indicates that all sequents of the proof tree are discharged.

The Editing Area   The editing area allows the user to enter parameters for proof commands. For example, in order for the user to add a new hypothesis, the user should enter this hypothesis into the editing area and then should click on the ᵃʰ button.

ML/PP and Hypotheses

ML   The ᵐˡ (mono-lemma) prover appears in the drop-down list under the button (pp) as M0, M1, M2, M3, and ML. The different configuration (e.g., M0) refer to the proof force of the ML prover. All hypotheses are passed to ML.

PP   The ᵖᵖ (predicate prover) appears in the drop-down list under the button (pp) as P0, P1, PP.

- The ᵖ⁰ prover uses all selected hypotheses in the Selected Hypotheses view.

- The ᵖ¹ prover performs a lasso operation on the selected hypotheses and the goal and uses the resulting hypotheses.

- The ᵖᵖ prover uses all hypotheses.

Auto Prover

The auto prover can be run by clicking the ♟ . This prover automatically applies all of the tactics that are predefined in the auto-tactic profile. Section 3.1.8 describes in detail how to configure the auto prover, and Section 3.4.3 gives an overview about what proof tactics are and which are available.

The Search Hypotheses View

By typing a string in the Proof Control view and pressing the Search Hypotheses (☞) button, all the hypotheses that have a character string in common with the one entered by the user in the editing area are shown in the Search Hypotheses view. For example, if we search for hypotheses containing the character string "cr", then after pressing the Search Hypothesis (☞) button on the Proof Control view, we obtain the windows as shown in Figure 3.34.

This view also integrates a "quick search" area (A), that allows us to search for hypotheses containing short character strings such as "cr", a search hypothesis button (B) that behaves the same as the button in the Proof Control view, a refresh button (C) that updates the window manually, and a drop down menu (D) to set up the preferences for the view.

By pressing return key or the button (B) (once a short string has been entered into the input area (A)), specific hypotheses can be found just as quickly as if we had used the Proof Control as described previously.

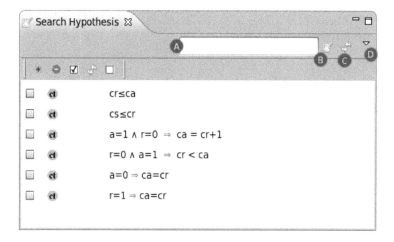

Figure 3.34: The Search Hypotheses View

The drop down menu (D) allows some preferences about the searched hypotheses to be set.

After we have changed preferences for the search, we might need to manually "update" the view with the button (C). By selecting the "Consider hidden hypotheses in search" option, we can view all the hypotheses are not selected in the Selected Hypotheses window.

To move hypotheses to the Selected Hypotheses window, select the desired hypotheses (using the check boxes) and press the ✴ button. Adding these hypotheses to the selected hypotheses means that they will be visible to the prover. They can then be used during the next interactive proof phase.

To remove hypotheses from the Search Hypotheses window, use the ⊖ button. This button also appears above the selected hypotheses and allows the user to remove any hypothesis from the Selected Hypotheses window.

The other button, situated to the left each hypotheses, is the ct button. Clicking on this will attempt a proof by contradiction. The effect is the same as if the hypothesis were in the Selected Hypotheses window.

The Cache Hypotheses View

This window allows the user to keep track of recently manipulated (i.e. used, removed, or selected) hypotheses for any PO. For example, when the user rewrites a hypothesis, the new hypothesis is selected, and the original hypothesis is deselected and put in the Cache Hypotheses window.

Operations similar to those in the Selected Hypotheses and Search Hypotheses views are also available for the cached hypotheses. It is possible to remove, select, and start a proof by contradiction (ct) in the Cache Hypotheses view as well. Interactive proof steps (e.g., rewriting) can also be carried out in the Cache Hypotheses view.

The Type Environment View

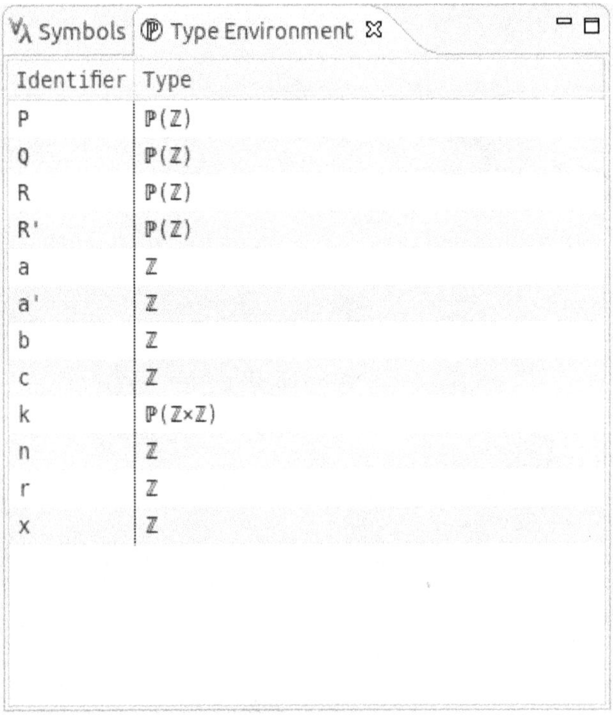

Figure 3.35: Type Environment View

This view 3.35 shows the type environment for the current node of the proof (free identifiers and their type). It is accessible through Window ⟩ Show View ⟩ Type Environment.

Proof Information View

This view displays information so that the user can relate a proof obligation to the model. For example, typical information for an event invariant preservation includes the event as well as the invariant in question. For instance, in Figure 3.36, the hyperlinks CreateToken and inv2 can be used to navigate to the containing machine.

Rule Details View

This view displays the information relating to a given proof tree node onto which a rule was applied. This information can be viewed by right clicking on any node in the proof tree and selecting Show Details... (see Figure 3.37).

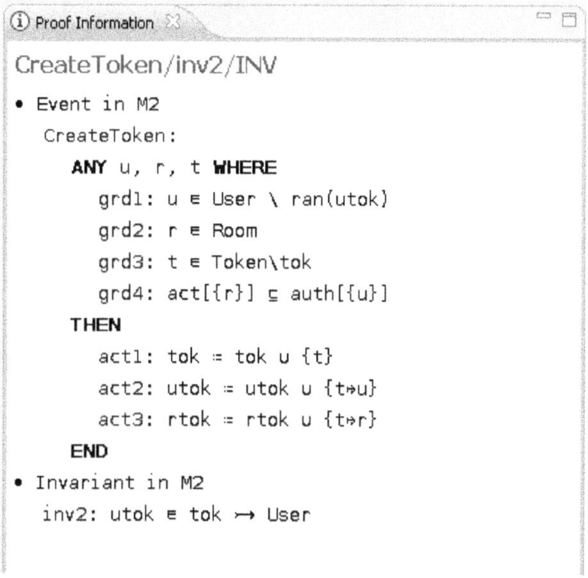

Proof Information
CreateToken/inv2/INV
• Event in M2
CreateToken:
ANY u, r, t WHERE
grd1: u ∈ User \ ran(utok)
grd2: r ∈ Room
grd3: t ∈ Token\tok
grd4: act[{r}] ⊆ auth[{u}]
THEN
act1: tok ≔ tok ∪ {t}
act2: utok ≔ utok ∪ {t↦u}
act3: rtok ≔ rtok ∪ {t↦r}
END
• Invariant in M2
inv2: utok ∈ tok ↣ User

Figure 3.36: Proof Information View

∀ hyp
Copy
Paste
Prune
Show details...
sl/ds

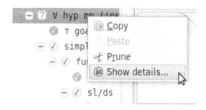

Figure 3.37: Open Rule Details View

By default, this view appears in the Fast View bar. If the window does not appear, click on the button in the Fast View bar to make this view visible. The Fast View bar is in the lower left corner of the Rodin workspace by default.

Figure 3.38 gives an overview of the Rule Details View.

We will now quickly cover all of the information that is displayed in this view. In this figure, the contents of the rule ∀ hyp mp are displayed. Here an input has been used to instantiate an hypothesis. The input that was used to instantiate the rule is shown on the line below Rule: ∀ hyp mp instantiated with:, and the hypothesis that was used by this rule is shown on the line below Input Sequent:. Furthermore, it is possible to view the antecedents (i.e. child proof tree nodes) created by this rule in detail and the actions (selection, deselection, etc.) that have been performed on the hypotheses.

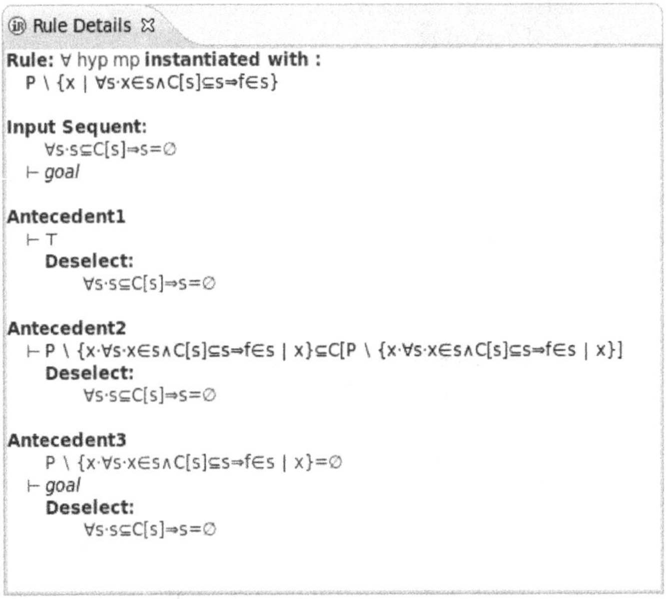

Figure 3.38: Rule Details View

Auto-tactic and Post-tactic

The auto-tactic automatically applies a combination (i.e. ordered list) of rewrite tactics, inference tactics and external provers to newly generated proof obligations. However, they can also be invoked by the user by clicking on the ♟ button in the Proof Control view. Note that the automatic application of the auto-prover can be quickly toggled with the Prove Automatically menu item available from the Project menu (See Figure 3.39).

The post-tactic is also a combination of rewrite tactics, inference tactics and external provers and is applied automatically after each interactive proof step. However, it can also be invoked manually by clicking on the ✐ button in the Proof Control view.

Note that the post-tactic can be disabled quickly by clicking on the ▽ button (marked with an A) of the Proof Control view (right upper corner) and then by deselecting the box next to the Enable post-tactic option (B) as shown in Figure 3.40.

Principles The ordered list of rewrite tactics, inference tactics and external provers that should be applied is called a profile. There are two default profiles. One is for auto-tactics and one is for post-tactics. These default profiles cannot be edited, but they can be duplicated for further modification by the user. The user can edit a profile and select it to run as automatic or post tactic. The idea is to have a set of available tactic profiles to be used as needed. Moreover, these

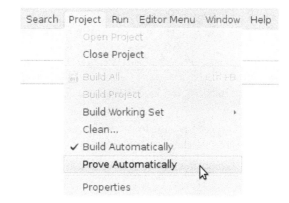

Figure 3.39: Toggle auto-prover via project menu

Figure 3.40: Proof Control view menu

edited profiles are saved within projects if they are defined at the project level, and they can be imported or exported if they are defined at a workspace level. This makes it easy to share the profiles.

There are two ways to run the automatic or post tactics:

- Manually by clicking on the ♔ button or the ✔ button in the Proof Control view to launch the auto-tactic (with the selected auto-tactic profile) and the post-tactic (with the selected post-tactic profile) respectively.

- Automatically if such preference is activated. (Auto-tactic will then run after each proof step and post-tactic will run after each step and rebuild). Post-tactics and auto-tactics only need to be activated in order to run automatically.

The user can separately define tactic profiles and assign them to post and auto tactics. Section 3.1.8 describes in detail how to configure auto- and post-tactics.

3.1.8 Preferences

Rodin provides several options to set the preferences of the Event-B editor. You can access the preferences via Window ⟩ Preferences ⟩ Event-B in the menu bar.

The following subsections describe the different preference options.

Appearance

This section provides settings for the Event-B editor appearance.

Colours and Fonts   The colour and fonts preference page allows you to set
the text and comment colour of the Event-B editor. Furthermore, it allows you
to turn the borders of the different fields in the Event-B editor on or off. Figure
3.41 shows the Colours and Fonts preference page.

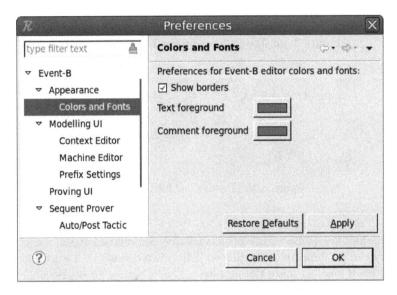

Figure 3.41: Colours and Fonts preferences

Modelling UI

The modelling UI preference pages allows you to customize the visible tabs of
the context and machine editor for the Event-B Structural Editor.

Prefix Settings

This page describes the default values that are used for the prefixes of the
different elements of contexts and machines. Note that prefixes are used for
automatic renaming when elements should be alphanumerically ordered in addition to when new elements are created.

Figure 3.42 shows that modifying prefixes on the workspace level or on the
project level will affect the names used at creation of new Event-B elements.
One can see that the prefixes for variables and invariants, which were originally

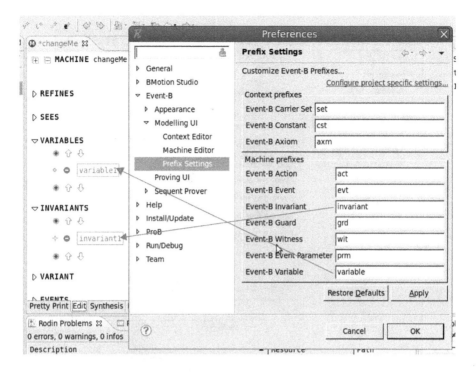

Figure 3.42: Prefix Settings

set to "var" or "inv", have been replaced by "variable" and "invariant". New elements are then named using those prefixes.

How to set prefixes Prefix settings can be accessed in two different ways depending on the scope of their application: via Window ⟩ Preferences ⟩ Event-B ⟩ Modelling UI ⟩ Prefix settings or via Rename ⟩ Customize prefixes....

Project specific settings The user can select profiles locally for a project. To do so, select the Properties item in the menu that pops up after right-clicking on a project in the Event-B Explorer. Then open the Prefix Settings tab and check the box to enable project specific settings. You can also click access this page by selecting Window ⟩ Preferences and then viewing the Event-B ⟩ Modelling UI ⟩ Prefix Settings page. Now select the Configure project specific settings link and select the desired project.

A window (see Figure 3.43) appears that allows a user to customize prefixes for a chosen project. On this page, the user can toggle the button Enable project specific settings:

- If this button is enabled, the prefixes used are those which are specified at this project level.

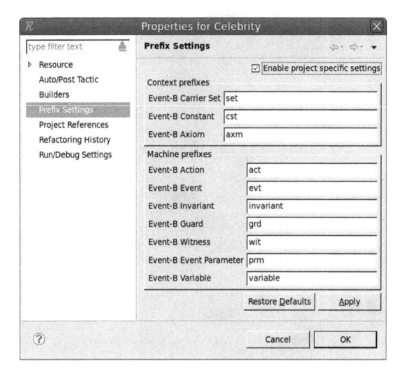

Figure 3.43: Project specific prefix settings

- If this button is not enabled, the prefixes used are those which are defined at the workspace level.

Sequent Prover / Auto/Post Tactic

Preferences for the selected auto and post tactic profile   There are multiple ways to access the preferences of the auto and post tactics at workspace or project scope:

from the Window ⟩ Preferences and then viewing the Event-B ⟩ Sequent Prover
    ⟩ Auto/Post Tactic page.

from the properties of a project to set project specific preferences for the
    Auto/Post Tactic.

from the drop-down menu in the Proof Control view.

The Proof Control view menu shows whether there are sequent prover preferences set for the project containing the current proof obligation 3.44 or not 3.45. Indeed, the command label in the menu tells if project specific settings are set, or if the workspace settings are considered. The command opens the corresponding Auto/Post Tactic page.

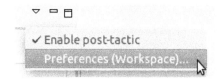

Figure 3.44: (a) direct access to the
Celebrity project specific settings

Figure 3.45: (b) no project settings
exist for the current PO, direct access to workspace settings

This section describes the Auto/Post Tactic tab of the Auto/Post Tactic preference page.

There are two scopes for the preferences of auto and post tactics: the
workspace level and the project level. Note that if the automatic application of
tactics is declared only at the workspace level, this option will also be set for
the project level.

To access these preferences, open the "Auto/Post Tactic" preference page
that can be found after Window ⟩ Preference ⟩ Sequent Prover.

Figure 3.46 shows the Auto/Post Tactic preference page.

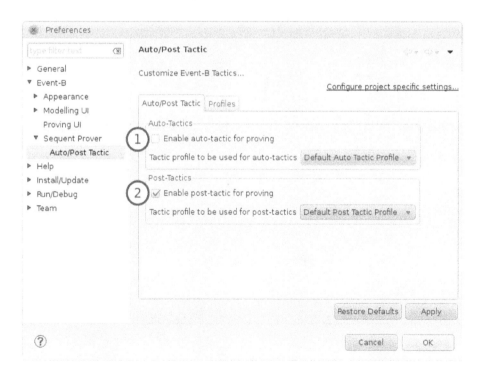

Figure 3.46: The "Auto/Post Tactic" preference page

The options shown by (1) and (2) allow you to activate/deactivate the automatic use of auto- and post-tactics. Here you can also choose the profile that should be used for auto- and post-tactics. Note that there is always a profile selected, and this profile can be changed regardless of whether the tactics are automatically launched or not because there is always a way to manually launch auto- and post-tactics. On the previously referenced figure, the Default Auto Tactic Profile is used for the automatic tactic, and the Default Post Tactic Profile is used for the post-tactic.

Preferences for available profiles   This section describes the Profile tab of the Auto/Post Tactic preference page.

Figure 3.47 shows the contents of the profile tab. There are two visible lists: a list of profiles on the left and the tactics or provers that make up these profiles (Profile Details). Here one can see the contents of the default Auto Tactic Profile.

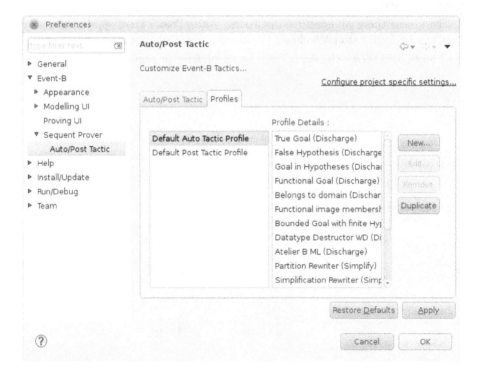

Figure 3.47: Selecting a profile for the Auto-Tactics

There are 4 buttons available to the user:

- New: to create a new profile "from scratch",

- Edit: to edit an existing profile (that can be edited),

- Remove: to delete a profile completely,

- Duplicate: to duplicate a selected profile for further slight modification.

Default profiles can not be edited nor removed. That is why these options are coloured in gray in the previously referenced figure.

Figure 3.48 shows the dialog available to edit or create a profile. For instance, here we create a profile named "MyFirstTacticProfile".

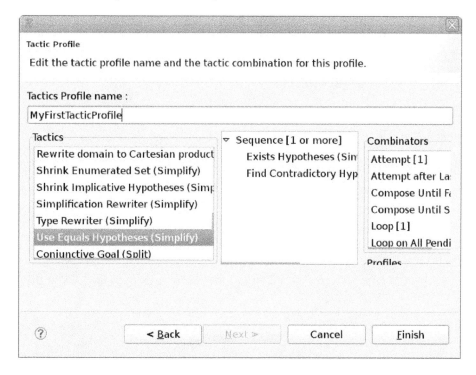

Figure 3.48: Selecting a profile for the Auto-Tactics

In the box labelled Tactics on the left, there is a list of all the different tactics that can be applied to a proof (tactics are explained in more detail in Section 3.4.3). In the box labelled Combinators (combinators are explained in more detail below in Section 3.1.8), there is a list of all the combinators that can be used for the proof tactic. To create your proof tactic, drag and drop one of the combinators into the center box. Then drag the proof tactics and drop them on top of the combinator that you just added. This will add the proof tactic to the combinator. You can also add more combinators or even other profiles (available in the Profiles box on the right side) to the combinator that you are working on. If you aren't certain what a proof tactic or combinator does, select it, and a description of the proof tactic or combinator will be be shown in the Description box that is shown in the lower right hand corner. If the tactic profile that you have created is valid, you will be able to hit the Finish button in the lower right hand corner in order to save it.

Project specific settings   The user can select profiles locally for each project. To do so, select the Auto/Post Tactic property page in the window that pops up when right-clicking on a project and selecting the Properties item, or selecting the Configure project specific settings link on the Auto/Post Tactic preference page. Figure 3.49 shows what this Auto/Post Tactic tab looks like.

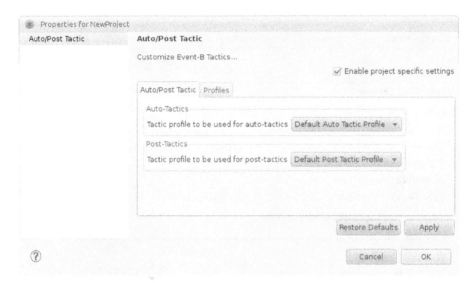

Figure 3.49: Auto/Post Tactic Tab for project specific settings for Auto/Post Tactic

Note that the enablement of automatic use of post and auto tactics is decided at the workspace level. Figure 3.50 shows the Profiles tab of the Auto/Post Tactic page for a project specific setting. At the project level, there is a contextual menu available via right click from the list of defined profiles.

This contextual menu offers two options to the user:

- Import Workspace Profiles retrieve all the defined profiles in the workspace.

- Export to Workspace Profiles push a selected profile up in the list of workspace profiles.

Preferences for Tactic Profiles

Introduction   The purpose of this section is to give a more detailed preferences to the user so he can build his own automated tactics. More precisely, the user should have a way to specify which parameters have to be passed to the reasoners and have a way to construct complex proof strategies.

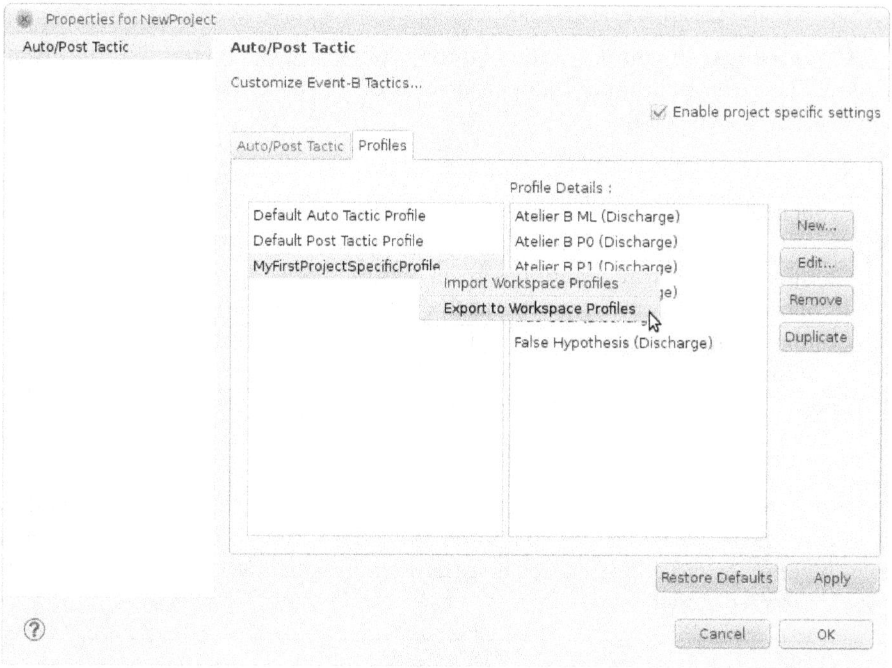

Figure 3.50: Profiles Tab for project specific settings for Auto/Post Tactic

User Documentation Here is the documentation about the current implementation of the Auto-tactic and Post-tactic preferences.

Tactic Combinators Tactic combinators can be used to construct complex proof strategies.

Historically, one combinator has existed since the beginning of auto tactic preferences: the "loop on all pending". It takes one or more tactics and loops them over every pending child until all tactic fail. Until Rodin 2.3 was released, this was the only combinator in Rodin. It is used on the configurable list of auto and post tactics. Rodin 2.3 is easier to configure because there are several other combinators and auto tactic editors.

The following is a list of combinators present by default.

One may notice the absence of child-specific combinator (i.e. combinators that apply tactic T1 on the first child, T2 on the second child, etc.) even though this kind of combinator exists in other provers. The reason is that these tactic profiles are applied automatically and therefore are only used in a general context. Provers with child-specific combinators are used to make manual proofs because they require proof-specific adaptation.

Composers   A composer combinator applies its given tactic(s) to the given node. The given node may be open or closed. It succeeds if at least 1 tactic application is successful.

Name	Arity	Description	Stops when
Sequence	1..n	applies given tactics in given order	all tactics have been applied
Compose until Success	1..n	applies given tactics in given order	a tactic application succeeds
Compose until failure	1..n	applies given tactics in given order	a tactic application fails
Loop	1	applies given tactic repeatedly	the child tactic application fails

Selectors   A selector combinator applies its given tactic to the set of nodes it selects. Selected nodes are computed from the given node. The given node may be open or closed. It succeeds if the tactic application is successful for at least 1 selected node.

Name	Arity	Selects
On all pending	1	all pending children of the given node (the given node itself if it is open)

Post Actions   A post actions applies its given tactic to the given node. The given node must be open (otherwise it fails). Then it performs a specific treatment which is guarded by a trigger condition.

Name	Arity	Trigger Condition	Post Action
Attempt	1	the given node still has pending children (subtree not closed)	prune proof tree at given node

Loop on All pending

$$loopOnAllPending(T_1 \ldots T_n)$$
$$\hat{=} \quad loop(onAllPending(composeUntilSuccess(T_1 \ldots T_n)))$$

Other Ideas   timeout: a post action of arity 1 (with duration as input): limits the time allocated for the tactic that it is applied to (fails after time has gone out)

limitDepth: a post action of arity 1 (with depth as input): limits the proof tree depth for the tactic that it is applied to (prevents tree from growing beyond a given depth)

3.2 Event-B's modelling notation

In Event-B, we have two types of components: contexts and machines. Here we describe briefly the different elements of a context or machine. We do not use a specific syntax for describing the components because the syntax is dependent on the editor that is used.

Proof obligations are generated to guarantee that certain properties of the modelled system are valid. We will explain here which proof obligations are generated, and we will list the goal and hypotheses that can be used when performing the proof for each one. This will be presented in the form:

	Description
Name	Label of the proof obligation (label refers to the label of the respective axiom/invariant/guard/etc.)
Goal	Goal that should be proved

Please note that Rodin often does not show a proof obligation if it is obviously true. If you expect to see a proof obligation that Rodin does not show, you can force that the proof obligation to be shown by changing the model temporarily so that the proof obligation cannot be automatically discharged. For example, you could introduce a division by zero to see the corresponding well-definedness condition.

We will begin by describing contexts and machines and how to prove their consistency. There are several locations where proof obligations for well-definedness conditions or predicates marked as theorems are raised. We summarized the proof obligations in separate sections. Well-definedness proof obligations are discussed in Section 3.2.5 and proof obligations for theorems are discussed in Section 3.2.6.

3.2.1 About the notation that we use

We denote a sequence of identifiers with $\mathbf{x} = x_1, \ldots, x_n$ and $\mathbf{x}' = x'_1, \ldots, x'_n$. As a convention, we use

- **c** for constants

- **v** and **w** for variables of an abstract or a concrete machine respectively

- **t** and **u** for parameters of an abstract or concrete machine respectively

- A for axioms

- I and J for the invariants of the abstract machines or concrete machine respectively

- G and H for the guards of the abstract events or concrete event respectively

3.2.2   Substitutions

We use the notation $P[E/x]$ for a substitution of all free occurrences of the variable x in P by the expression E. Several substitutions can be performed simultaneously with $P(E_1/x_1, \ldots, E_n/x_n)$. In particular, we use the syntax $P[\mathbf{x}'/\mathbf{x}]$ to denote the substitution of each identifier x in the sequence $\mathbf{x}$ by x'. For more information on free identifiers, see Section 3.3.1.

Examples:

- $(x > y)[5 + 2/y]$ corresponds to the predicate $(x > 5 + 2)$.

- $(x > y)[2 \cdot y/x, 5 + 2/y]$ corresponds to the predicate $(2 \cdot y > 5 + 2)$.

- $(\exists x \cdot x \in S \land x > y)[2 \cdot y/x, 5 + 2/y]$ corresponds to the predicate $(\exists x \cdot x \in S \land x > 5 + 2)$, because the x is a quantified variable (i.e. it is not a free variable).

- For a sequence $\mathbf{v} = v_1, v_2, v_3$ the predicate $(v_1 \subseteq v_2 \land v_3 \in v_1)[\mathbf{v}'/\mathbf{v}]$ corresponds to $(v_1' \subseteq v_2' \land v_3' \in v_1')$.

3.2.3   Contexts

A context describes the static part of a model. It consists of

- Carrier sets

- Constants

- Axioms

- Extended contexts

Carrier Sets

A new data type can be declared by adding its name – an identifier – to the *Sets* section. The identifier must be unique, i.e. it must not have been already declared as a constant or set in the current context or an extended context. The identifier is then implicitly introduced as a new constant (see below) that represents the set of all elements of the type.

A common pattern for declaring enumerated sets (sets where all elements are explicitly given) is to use the partition operator. If we want to specify a set S with elements $e_1, \ldots, e_n$, we declare S as a set, $e_1, \ldots, e_n$ as constants and add the axiom $partition(S, e_1, \ldots, e_n)$.

Extending a context

Other contexts can be extended by adding their name to the *Extends* section.

The resulting context consists of all constants and axioms of all extended contexts and the extending context itself. Thus for a context or machine that extends or sees the contexts, it makes no difference where a constant or axiom is declared.

Extending two contexts which declare a constant or set using the same identifier will result in an error.

Constants and axioms

Constants can be declared by adding their unique name (an identifier) to the *Constants* section. An axiom must also be in place from which the type of the constant can be inferred. We denote the sequence of all constants with $\mathbf{c}$.

An axiom is a statement that is assumed to be true in the rest of the model. Each axiom consists of a label and a predicate A. All free identifiers in A must be constants.

Axioms can be marked as theorems. The proof obligation that are then generated are described in Section 3.2.6. The validity of a theorem can be proven from the axioms that have already been declared.

The well-definedness of axioms must be proven if an axiom contains a well-definedness condition (3.2.5).

3.2.4 Machines

A machine describes the dynamic behavior of a model by means of variables whose values are changed by events.

There are two basic things that must be proven for a machine:

1. The machine must be consistent, i.e. it should never reach a state which violates the invariant.

2. The machine is a correct refinement, i.e. its behavior must correspond to any machines that it refines.

Refinement and Abstract machines

A machine can refine at most one other machine. We refer to the refined machine as the abstract machine and refer to the refinement as the concrete machine. More generally, a machine M_0 can be refined by machine M_1, M_1 refined by M_2 and so on. The most concrete refinement would be M_n.

Basically, a refinement consists of two aspects:

1. The concrete machine's state is connected to the state of the abstract machine. To do this, an invariant is used to relate abstract and concrete variables. This invariant is called a *gluing invariant*.

2. Each abstract event can be refined by one or more concrete events.

The full invariant of the machine consists of both abstract and concrete invariants. The invariants are accumulated during refinements.

How to use Refinement: Refinement can be used to subsequently add complexity to the model - this is called superposition refinement (or horizontal refinement). It can also be used to add detail to data structures – this is called data refinement (or vertical refinement). We've seen both types of refinement in the tutorial (Chapter 2).

Seeing a context

If the machine sees a context, the sets and constants declared in the context can be used in all predicates and expressions. The conjunction of axioms A can be used as hypotheses in the proofs.

Variables and invariants

Variables can be declared by adding their unique name (an identifier) to the *Variables* section. The type of the variables must be inferable by the invariants of the machine. We denote the variables of the abstract machines $M_1, \ldots, M_{n-1}$ with a **v** and the variables of the concrete machine with a **w**.

An invariant is a statement that must be valid at each state of the machine. Each invariant i consists of a label and a predicate I_i. An invariant can refer to the constants as well as the variables of the concrete and all abstract machines.

We write I to denote the conjunction of all invariants of the abstract machines and J for the conjunction of the concrete machine's invariant.

Invariants that are marked as theorems derive their correctness from the preservation of other invariants, so their preservation does not need to be proven. The proof obligation can be found in Section 3.2.6.

If an invariant contains a well-definedness condition, a corresponding proof obligation is generated (3.2.5).

Common variables between machines With some restrictions, the abstract variables **v** and concrete variables **w** can have variables in common. If a variable v is declared in a machine M_i, it can be re-used in the direct refinement M_{i+1}. In that case, it is assumed that the values of the abstract and concrete variable are always equal. To ensure this, special proof obligations are generated (3.2.4). Once a variable disappears in a refinement, i.e. it is not declared in machine M_{i+2}, it cannot be re-introduced in a later refinement.

Events

A possible state change for a machine is defined by an event. The condition under which an event can be executed is given by a guard. The event's action describes how the new and old state relate to each other.

Events occur atomically (i.e. one event happens at a time) and to a new state. Two events never happen at the same time. Time is also not factored into the execution of the event.

An event has the following elements:

- Name

- Parameters

- Guards

- Witnesses

- Actions

- Status (ordinary, convergent or anticipated): The status is used for termination proofs (see Section 3.2.4 for details).

An event can refine one or more events of an abstract machine. To keep things simple, we will first consider events with only one refined event. If there are several refinement steps, we describe events from the refined machines as abstract events and the event from the concrete machine as the concrete event. For example, if an event E_1 is refined by E_2 and E_2 is refined by $E3$, we call E_1 and E_2 the abstract events and E_3 the concrete event. Likewise, if we refer to the parameters of the abstract events, we mean all the parameters of all the abstract events (e.g., the parameters of E_1 and E_2).

Parameters An event can have an arbitrary number of *parameters*. Their names must be unique, i.e. there must be no constant or variable with the same name. The types of the parameters must be declared in the guards of the event. We denote the parameters of all abstract events with **t** and the parameters of the concrete event with **u**.

Similarly to variables, an event can have parameters in common with the event it refines. If the refined event has a parameter t which is not a parameter of the refinement, a witness W_t for the abstract parameter must be specified (3.2.4). All free identifiers in W_t must be either constants, concrete or abstract variables, concrete parameters or the abstract parameter t.

Guards Each *guard* consist of a label and a predicate H. All free identifiers in H must be constants, concrete variables or concrete parameters. Variables or parameters of abstract machines are not accessible in a guard.

We write G for the conjunction of all guards of all abstract events.

Like axioms and invariants, guards can also be marked as theorems. The proof obligation can be found in Section 3.2.6. If the guard contains WD-conditions, a proof obligation is generated. See Section 3.2.5 for the proof obligation.

Actions An action is composed of a label and an assignment. Section 3.3.8 gives an overview of how they are assigned. They can be put into two groups: deterministic and non-deterministic assignments. Each assignment affects one or more concrete variables.

If an event has more than one action, they are executed in parallel. An error will occur if a new value is assigned to a variable in more than one action. All variables to which no new value is assigned keep the same value in new and old state.

We now define the before-after-predicate $\mathcal{T}$ of the actions together. Let $Q_1, \ldots, Q_n$ be the before-after-predicate of the event's assignments. Let $x_1, \ldots, x_k$ be the variables that are assigned by any action of the event. Let $y_1, \ldots, y_l$ be the variables of the concrete machine that are *not* modified by any of the event's actions (i.e. $\mathbf{w} = x_1, \ldots, x_k, y_1, \ldots, y_l$). Then the before-after-predicate of the concrete event is $\mathcal{T} = Q_1 \wedge \ldots \wedge Q_n \wedge y_1 = y_1' \wedge \ldots \wedge y_l = y_l'$.

Please note that Rodin optimizes proof obligations when a before-after-predicate is a hypothesis. x' is replaced directly by x when x is not changed by the event and replaced by E when E is assigned to x deterministically.

Witnesses   Witnesses are composed of a label and a predicate that establishes a link between the values of the variables and parameters of the concrete and abstract events. Most of the time, this predicate is a simple equality.

    Unlike other elements in Event-B that have a label, the label of a witness has a meaning and cannot be chosen arbitrarily.

If the user does not specify a witness, Rodin uses the default witness $\top$.

Witnesses are necessary in the following circumstances:

- The abstract event has a parameter p that is not a parameter of the concrete event. In this case, the label of the witness must be p, and the witness has the form W_p. All identifiers of W_p must be either constants, concrete or abstract variables, primed concrete variables (i.e. v' for each concrete variable v), concrete parameters or the abstract parameter p.

- The abstract event assigns non-deterministically (using $:\in$ or $:|$) a value to a variable x that is not a variable of the concrete machine. In this case, the label of the witness must be x', the witness has the form $W_{x'}$. All identifiers of W_p must be either constants, concrete or abstract variables, primed concrete variables (i.e. v' for each concrete variable v), concrete parameters or the primed abstract variable x'. x' denotes the new value of x.

We denote the conjunction of all witnesses of an event with W.

The feasibility of the witness must be proven, i.e. that there is actually a value for which the predicate holds.

Witness feasibility for a parameter p	
Name	eventlabel/p/WFIS
Goal	$A \wedge I \wedge J \wedge H$ $\Rightarrow \exists p \cdot W_p$

Witness feasibility for an abstract variable x	
Name	eventlabel/x'/WFIS
Goal	$A \wedge I \wedge J \wedge H \wedge \mathcal{T}$ $\Rightarrow \exists x' \cdot W_{x'}$

A witness may contain well-definedness conditions. See 3.2.5 for the corresponding proof obligation.

Initialisation   The initialisation of a machine is given by a special event called *INITIALISATION*. Unlike other events, the initialisation must not contain guards and parameters. The actions must not make use of variable values before the initialisation event occurs. All variables must have a value assigned to them. If there is no assignment for the variable x, Rodin assumes a default assignment of the form $x :| \top$.

Ensuring machine consistency   The following proof obligations are generated for events:

The assignment of each action must be well-defined when the event is enabled. See 3.2.5 for the corresponding proof obligation.

If the event's guard is enabled, every action must be feasible. This is trivially true in the case of the deterministic assignments. For a non-deterministic assignment a, the feasibility $\mathcal{F}(a)$ must be proven. The feasibility operator $\mathcal{F}$ is described in Section 3.3.8.

	Action feasibility
Name	eventlabel/actionlabel/FIS
Goal	$A \wedge I \wedge J \wedge H \wedge W_p \wedge S$ $\Rightarrow \mathcal{F}(a)$

For each invariant J_i with the label invlabel that contains a variable affected by the assignment, it must be proven that the invariant still is still valid for the new values.

	Invariant preservation
Name	eventlabel/invlabel/INV
Goal	$A \wedge I \wedge J \wedge H \wedge W_v \wedge \mathcal{T}$ $\Rightarrow J_i[\mathbf{v'}/\mathbf{v}, \mathbf{w'}/\mathbf{w}]$

Rodin simplifies this proof obligations by replacing x' with x for variables that are not changed and x' by E for variables that are assigned by a deterministic $(x := E)$ assignment.

There are special proof obligations generated for the initialisation event:

	Action feasibility (in the initialisation)
Name	INITIALISATION/actionlabel/FIS
Goal	$A \wedge W \wedge \mathcal{T} \Rightarrow \mathcal{F}(a)$

	Invariant establishment
Name	INITIALISATION/invlabel/INV
Goal	$A \wedge W \wedge \mathcal{T} \Rightarrow I_i[\mathbf{v'}/\mathbf{v}, \mathbf{w'}/\mathbf{w}]$

Ensuring a correct refinement

An event can refine one or more events of the abstract machine. We first consider the refinement of only one event. For refining more than one event (i.e. merging events), please refer below to Section 3.2.4.

If an event does not refine an abstract event, it is implicitly assumed that it refines *skip*, the event that is always enabled (i.e. its guard is $\top$) and does nothing (i.e. all variables keep their values).

Guard strengthening A concrete event must only be enabled if the abstract event is enabled. This condition is called *guard strengthening*. For each abstract guard G_i with label guardlabel, the following proof obligation is generated:

	Guard strengthening
Name	eventname/guardlabel/GRD
Goal	$A \wedge I \wedge J \wedge H \wedge W_p$ $\Rightarrow G_i$

Action simulation If an abstract event's action i (with before-after predicate Q_i) assigns a value to a variable that is also declared in the concrete machine, it must be proven that the abstract event's behaviour corresponds to the concrete behaviour. The behaviour of the concrete event is given by the concrete before-after-predicate $\mathcal{T}$, and the relevant abstract behaviour is given by the before-after-predicate Q_i. The relation between abstract and concrete event is specified by witnesses.

	Action simulation
Name	eventname/actionlabel/SIM
Goal	$A \wedge I \wedge J \wedge H \wedge W \wedge \mathcal{T}$ $\Rightarrow Q_i$

When the assignments are deterministic or the witnesses are equations, the proof obligation can usually be simplified by Rodin.

Preserved variables If x is a variable of both the abstract and concrete machine and the concrete event assigns a value to x but the abstract event does not, it must be proven that the variable's value does not change. Let Q_i be the before-after-predicate of the action that changes x.

	Equality of a preserved variable x
Name	eventname/x/EQL
Goal	$A \wedge I \wedge J \wedge H \wedge Q_i$ $\Rightarrow x' = x$

Merging events

Refining more than one abstract event by a single event is called *merging* of events. To merge events, two conditions must be taken into account.

- If two abstract events declare the same parameter, they must be of the same type.

- All abstract events must have identical actions.

Instead of the guard strengthening proof obligation, the following proof obligation is created with $G_1, \ldots, G_n$ as the abstract guards of the merged events and $\mathbf{t}_1, \ldots, \mathbf{t}_n$ as their parameters.

Guard strengthening (merge)	
Name	eventlabel/MRG
Goal	$A \wedge I \wedge J \wedge H \wedge W \wedge \mathcal{T}$ $\Rightarrow G_1 \vee \ldots \vee G_n$

The other proof obligations are the same as for refining a single event. Also, the same rules for defining witnesses apply.

Extending events

Instead of refining another event, an event can *extend* it. In this case the refined event will implicitly have all the parameters, guards and actions of the refined event. It can have additional parameters, guards and actions. The same effect can be achieved by manually copying the parameters, guards and actions.

This is especially useful when additional features are gradually introduced into a model by refinement (also called "superposition refinement").

Termination

Event-B makes it possible to prove how an event will terminate. Termination means that a chosen set of events are enabled only a finite number of times before an event that is not marked as terminating occurs. To support proofs for termination, a *variant* V can be specified in a model. All free identifiers in V must be constants or concrete variables. A variant is an expression that is either numeric ($V \in \mathbb{Z}$) or a finite set ($V \in \mathbb{P}(\alpha)$, where α is an arbitrary type).

Events can be marked as:

ordinary when the event may occur arbitrarily often and does not underlie any restrictions regarding the variant.

convergent when the event must decrease the variant.

anticipated when the event must not increase the variant.

Informally, termination is proven by stating that the convergent events strictly decrease the variant which has a lower bound. If a model contains a convergent event, a variant must be specified. If only anticipated events are declared, it is sufficient to create a default constant variant so that all anticipated events do not increase the variant. When an event is marked as anticipated, one must just prove that the event does not increase the variant. The proof of termination is then delayed to the refinements of the anticipated event. A refinement of an anticipated event must be either anticipated or convergent.

If the convergence of an event is proven, the convergence of its refinements is also guaranteed due to guard strengthening.

A variant must be well-defined. The corresponding well-definedness proof obligations can be found in Section 3.2.5. The following other proof obligations are generated:

Numeric variant   If the variant is numeric, an anticipated or convergent event must only be enabled when the variant is non-negative.

	Numeric variant is a natural number
Name	eventlabel/NAT
Goal	$A \wedge I \wedge J \wedge G \wedge H$ $\Rightarrow V \in \mathbb{N}$

A convergent event must decrease the variant

	Decreasing of a numeric variant (convergent event)
Name	eventlabel/VAR
Goal	$A \wedge I \wedge J \wedge G \wedge H \wedge \mathcal{T}$ $\Rightarrow V[\mathbf{w'}/\mathbf{w}] < V$

and an anticipated event must not increase the variant.

	Decreasing of a numeric variant (anticipated event)
Name	eventlabel/VAR
Goal	$A \wedge I \wedge J \wedge G \wedge H \wedge \mathcal{T}$ $\Rightarrow V[\mathbf{w'}/\mathbf{w}] \leq V$

Set variant   If the variant is a set t, it must be proven that the set is always finite:

	Decreasing of a variant (anticipated event)
Name	FIN
Goal	$A \wedge I \wedge J$ $\Rightarrow \text{finite}(V)$

A convergent event must remove elements from the set

	Decreasing of a set variant (convergent event)
Name	eventlabel/VAR
Goal	$A \wedge I \wedge J \wedge G \wedge H \wedge \mathcal{T}$ $\Rightarrow V[\mathbf{w}'/\mathbf{w}] \subset V$

and an anticipated event must not add elements.

	Decreasing of a set variant (anticipated event)
Name	eventlabel/VAR
Goal	$A \wedge I \wedge J \wedge G \wedge H \wedge \mathcal{T}$ $\Rightarrow V[\mathbf{w}'/\mathbf{w}] \subseteq V$

3.2.5 Well-definedness proof obligations

There are several locations where well-definedness proof obligations can be created. The mathematical notation of the well-definedness conditions of each operator are defined by the $\mathcal{L}$-operator (3.3.1).

For well-definedness conditions, the order of axioms, invariants and guards is important. Well-definedness conditions are not usually shown in Rodin if they are trivial ($\top$).

Axioms For an axiom A_w, A_b denotes (the conjunction of) all axioms declared in extended contexts and the axioms already declared in the current context before the axiom in question.

	Well-definedness of an axiom
Name	label/WD
Goal	$A_b \Rightarrow \mathcal{L}(A_w)$

Invariants For an invariant J_w, J_b denotes (the conjunction of) all the model's invariants declared before the theorem.

	Well-definedness of an invariant
Name	label/WD
Goal	$A \wedge I \wedge J_b \Rightarrow \mathcal{L}(J_w)$

Guards For an invariant H_w, H_b denotes (the conjunction of) all the model's invariants declared before the theorem.

	Well-definedness of a guard
Name	eventname/guardlabel/WD
Goal	$A \wedge I \wedge J \wedge H_b \Rightarrow \mathcal{L}(H_w)$

Witnesses   A witness W may contain well-definedness conditions.

Well-definedness of a witness
Name   eventlabel/witnesslabel/WWD
Goal $A \wedge I \wedge J \wedge \mathcal{T} \Rightarrow \mathcal{L}(W)$

Actions   The assignment a of each action with the label actionlabel in an event must be well-defined.

Well-definedness of an action
Name   eventlabel/actionlabel/WD
Goal $A \wedge I \wedge J \wedge G \wedge H \Rightarrow \mathcal{L}(a)$

Variants   A variant V must be well-defined.

Well-definedness of a variant
Name   VWD
Goal $A \wedge J \Rightarrow \mathcal{L}(V)$

3.2.6   Theorems

Axioms, invariants and guards can be marked as theorems. This means that the validity of the theorems must be proven from the axioms, invariants or guards declared before the theorem.

Sometimes an axiom/invariant/guard marked as theorem is also called a *derived* axiom/invariant/guard.

Axioms   For an axiom A_{thm}, A_b denotes (the conjunction of) all axioms declared in extended contexts and the axioms already declared in the current context before the axiom in question.

An axiom as theorem
Name   label/THM
Goal $A_b \Rightarrow A_{thm}$

Invariants   For an invariant J_{thm}, J_b denotes (the conjunction of) all the model's invariants declared before the theorem.

An invariant as theorem
Name   label/THM
Goal $A \wedge I \wedge J_b \Rightarrow J_{thm}$

Guards   For a guard H_{thm}, H_b denotes (the conjunction of) all the event's guards declared before the theorem.

A guard as theorem
Name   label/THM
Goal $A \wedge I \wedge J \wedge H_b \Rightarrow H_{thm}$

generated in contexts		
well-definedness of an axiom	label/WD	3.2.5
axiom as theorem	label/THM	3.2.6
generated for machine consistency		
well-definedness of an invariant	label/WD	3.2.5
invariant as theorem	label/THM	3.2.6
well-definedness of a guard	event/guardlabel/WD	3.2.5
guard as theorem	event/guardlabel/THM	3.2.6
well-definedness of an action	event/actionlabel/WD	3.2.5
feasibility of a non-det. action	event/actionlabel/FIS	3.2.4
invariant preservation	event/invariantlabel/INV	3.2.4
generated for refinements		
guard strengthening	event/abstract_grd_label/GRD	3.2.4
action simulation	event/abstract_act_label/SIM	3.2.4
equality of a preserved variable	event/variable/EQL	3.2.4
guard strengthening (merge)	event/MRG	3.2.4
well definedness of a witness	event/identifier/WWD	3.2.5
feasibility of a witness	event/identifier/WFIS	3.2.4
generated for termination proofs		
well definedness of a variant	VWD	3.2.5
finiteness for a set variant	FIN	3.2.4
natural number for a numeric variant	event/NAT	3.2.4
decreasing of variant	event/VAR	3.2.4

Table 3.1: Generated Proof Obligations

3.2.7 Generated proof obligations

Table 3.1 shows a brief overview about the different proof obligations that are generated. The user can use this table to identify a specific proof obligation. For further information, a reference to the relevant reference section is provided.

3.2.8 Visibility of identifiers

Expressions and predicates are comprised of certain Event-B elements. The following table describes the elements that each predicate or expression use:

	sets	constants	variables		parameters	
			concrete	abstract	concrete	abstract
axiom	×	×				
invariant	×	×	×	×		
variant	×	×	×	×		
guard	×	×	×		×	
witness*	×	×	×	×	×	×
action*	×	×	×		×	

However, expressions and predicates can only use elements that are identified within a specific scope:

Sets Sets can be used when they are defined in the context (in case of an axiom) or in a seen context. If a context extends another context, the sets of the extended context are treated as if they are defined in the extending context.

Constants Constants can be used when they are defined in the context (in the case of an axiom) or in a seen context.

Concrete Variables Concrete variables that are defined in the machine itself can be used.

Abstract Variables Abstract variables that are defined in an abstract machine can be used.

Concrete Parameters Parameters that are defined in the event itself can be used.

Abstract Parameters Parameters that are defined in an abstract event can be used.

* Witnesses and actions have additional elements in their scope. Section 3.2.4 provides more information about witnesses, and Section 3.3.8 explains the scope for actions that have different types of assignments in further detail.

3.3 Mathematical Notation

3.3.1 Introduction

In the following section, we use sans serif letters like a, A, b, B, ... as place-holders for arbitrary expressions instead of a, A, b, B which represent Event-B identifiers. For example, the e and S in e $\in$ S could be a placeholder for $5 + 2$ and $\mathbb{N}$.

We use the A $\hat{=}$ B to state that an expression, predicate or assignment A can be equivalently rewritten as B if A's well-definedness condition is fulfilled. We have tried to find a balance between having a precise and concise description for all Event-B's mathematical components and having a text that is still easily readable. Many of the operators can be expressed using other, simpler constructs. Other, like equality (=) or universal quantification ($\forall$) are simply described with natural language.

When we introduce new identifiers while expressing an operator (e.g. by using a set comprehension), we assume that the new identifier does not occur free in the rewritten expressions (see Section 3.3.1 for more information on free identifiers).

 For a concise summary of the Event-B mathematical toolkit, download the four-page Event-B Cheat Sheet[3]. We would like to thank Ken Robinson for making it available.

Data types

In Event-B we have 3 kinds of basic data types:

- $\mathbb{Z}$ is the set of all integers.

- BOOL is the set of Booleans. It has two elements BOOL = {TRUE, FALSE}.

- Users can define carrier sets. These are defined in the *Sets* section of a context. Carrier sets are never empty. There is no other assumption made about carrier sets unless it is stated explicitly as an axiom.

From all data types α, β, two other kinds of data types can be constructed:

- $\mathbb{P}(\alpha)$ contains the sets of elements of α.

- $\alpha \times \beta$ is the set of pairs where the first element is of type α and the second element is of type β.

Expressions that are constructed by the rules above are called *type expressions*.

---

[3]The URL of the resource is: `http://handbook.event-b.org/current/files/EventB-Summary.pdf`

A note about the notation   We use the Greek letters α, β, γ, ... to represent arbitrary data types. For an expression E, we write $E \in \alpha$ to state that E is of type α. In the following descriptions of Event-B's mathematical constructs, we will describe the types of all constructs and their components.

For example, we will describe the maplet $E \mapsto F$ whose type is defined by $E \mapsto F \in \alpha \times \beta$ with $E \in \alpha$ and $F \in \beta$. We do not restrict the types of α and β.

For predicates, we simply describe the data types of their components. The predicate itself does not have a type. For example, consider the components' types for the equality of two expressions $E = F$: $E \in \alpha$ and $F \in \alpha$. By stating that E and F are both of type α, we express that both expressions must have the same type but do not make any further assumptions about their types.

Well-definedness

A predicate which describes the condition under which an expression or predicate in Event-B can be safely evaluated is the well-definedness condition. An example with integer division makes this clear: The expression $x \div y$ only makes sense when $y \neq 0$.

Well-definedness conditions are usually used for well-definedness proof obligations (3.2.5).

In Rodin, the $\mathcal{L}$-operator defines which well-defined condition a predicate or expression has. When applied to the above example, integer division can be formatted as follows: $\mathcal{L}(x \div y) \,\widehat{=}\, y \neq 0$.

In the following sections, we state for each mathematical construct what the well-definedness conditions are. In many cases, this is just the conjunction of the well-definedness conditions for the different syntactical parts of a construct.

> The $\mathcal{L}$-operator cannot be expressed in Event-B itself. It is only used to describe Event-B's concept of well-definedness and how the well-definedness proof obligations are generated.

Free identifiers

Free identifiers in predicates and expressions are those identifiers which are used but not introduced by quantifiers. More formally, we define the set of free identifiers *Free*(E) of an expression or predicate E recursively as follows:

Expression / Predicate	Free identifiers
Identifier x	$\{x\}$
Integer n	$\varnothing$
$\top$ $\bot$ BOOL TRUE FALSE $\varnothing$ id prj_1 prj_2 $\mathbb{Z}$ $\mathbb{N}$ $\mathbb{N}_1$	$\varnothing$
$\neg A$ bool(A) $\mathbb{P}(A)$ $\mathbb{P}_1(A)$ finite(A) card(A) union(A) inter(A) A^{-1} dom(A) ran(A) $-A$ min(A) max(A)	*Free*(A)
$A \wedge B$ $A \vee B$ $A \Rightarrow B$ $A \Leftrightarrow B$ $A = B$ $A \neq B$ $A \in B$ $A \notin B$ $A \subseteq B$ $A \nsubseteq B$ $A \subset B$ $A \not\subset B$ $A \cup B$ $A \cap B$ $A \setminus B$ $A \times B$ $A \leftrightarrow B$ $A \nleftrightarrow B$ $A \leftrightarrow\!\!\!\rightarrow B$ $A \nleftrightarrow\!\!\!\rightarrow B$ $A \lhd B$ $A \vartriangleleft B$ $A \rhd B$ $A \vartriangleright B$ $A ; B$ $A \circ B$ $A \lhd\!\!\!- B$ $A \| B$ $A \otimes B$ $A[B]$ $A \nrightarrow B$ $A \rightarrow B$ $A \rightarrowtail B$ $A \rightarrowtail B$ $A \twoheadrightarrow B$ $A \twoheadrightarrow B$ $A \rightarrowtail\!\!\!\rightarrow B$ $A(B)$ $A + B$ $A - B$ $A \cdot B$ $A \div B$ $A \bmod B$ $A \hat{} B$ $A \circ\!\!\circ B$	*Free*(A) $\cup$ *Free*(B)
$\{E_1, \ldots, E_n\}$ partition$(E_1, \ldots, E_n)$	*Free*$(E_1) \cup \ldots \cup$ *Free*(E_n)
$\forall ids \cdot P$ $\exists ids \cdot P$	*Free*(P) $\setminus$ *ids*
$\{ ids \cdot P \mid E \}$ $\bigcup ids \cdot P \mid E$ $\bigcap ids \cdot P \mid E$	(*Free*(P) $\cup$ *Free*(E)) $\setminus$ *ids*
$\{ E \mid P \}$ $\bigcup E \mid P$ $\bigcap E \mid P$	*Free*(P) $\setminus$ *Free*(E)

Structure of the subsections

The following reference subsections will have the form the form:

math. Symbol — **ASCII representation** — Name of the operator

... — ... — ...

Description A short description of what the operator does

Definition A formal definition of what the operator does

Types A description of the types of all arguments and, if the operation is an expression, the expression's type

WD A description of the well-definedness conditions using the $\mathcal{L}$ operator

Feasibility Non-deterministic assignments may have feasibility conditions. These are used in the proof obligations of an event (3.2.4).

Example For some constructs, an example is provided to clarify their use.

3.3.2   Predicates

Logical primitives

$$\top \ — \ \texttt{true} \ — \ \text{True}$$
$$\bot \ — \ \texttt{false} \ — \ \text{False}$$

Description The predicates $\top$ and $\bot$ are the predicates that are true and false respectively.

WD $\mathcal{L}(\top) \mathrel{\hat{=}} \top$
$\mathcal{L}(\bot) \mathrel{\hat{=}} \top$

Logical operators

$$\wedge \ — \ \texttt{\&} \ — \ \text{Conjunction}$$
$$\vee \ — \ \texttt{or} \ — \ \text{Disjunction}$$
$$\Rightarrow \ — \ \texttt{=>} \ — \ \text{Implication}$$
$$\Leftrightarrow \ — \ \texttt{<=>} \ — \ \text{Equivalence}$$
$$\neg \ — \ \texttt{not} \ — \ \text{Negation}$$

Description These are the usual logical operators.

Definition The following truth tables describe the behaviours of these operators:

P	Q	$P \wedge Q$	$P \vee Q$	$P \Rightarrow Q$	$P \Leftrightarrow Q$
$\bot$	$\bot$	$\bot$	$\bot$	$\top$	$\top$
$\bot$	$\top$	$\bot$	$\top$	$\top$	$\bot$
$\top$	$\bot$	$\bot$	$\top$	$\bot$	$\bot$
$\top$	$\top$	$\top$	$\top$	$\top$	$\top$

P	$\neg$P
$\bot$	$\top$
$\top$	$\bot$

Types All arguments are predicates.

WD Please note that the operators $\wedge$ and $\vee$ are not commutative because their well-definedness conditions distinguish between the first and second argument. Therefore, if their arguments have well-definedness conditions, the order matters. For example, $x \neq 0 \wedge y \div x = 3$ is always well-defined, but $y \div x = 3 \wedge x \neq 0$ still has the well-definedness condition $x \neq 0$.

$\mathcal{L}(P \wedge Q) \mathrel{\hat{=}} \mathcal{L}(P) \wedge (P \Rightarrow \mathcal{L}(Q))$
$\mathcal{L}(P \vee Q) \mathrel{\hat{=}} \mathcal{L}(P) \wedge (P \vee \mathcal{L}(Q))$
$\mathcal{L}(P \Rightarrow Q) \mathrel{\hat{=}} \mathcal{L}(P) \wedge (P \Rightarrow \mathcal{L}(Q))$
$\mathcal{L}(P \Leftrightarrow Q) \mathrel{\hat{=}} \mathcal{L}(P) \wedge \mathcal{L}(Q)$
$\mathcal{L}(\neg(P)) \mathrel{\hat{=}} \mathcal{L}(P)$

Quantified predicates

$$\forall \quad - \quad ! \quad - \quad \text{Universal quantification}$$
$$\exists \quad - \quad \# \quad - \quad \text{Existential quantification}$$

Description The universal quantification $\forall x_1, \ldots, x_n \cdot P$ is true if P is satisfied for all possible values of $x_1 \ldots, x_n$. A usual pattern for quantification is $\forall x_1 \ldots, x_n \cdot P_1 \Rightarrow P_2$ where P_1 is used to specify the types of the identifiers.

The existential quantification $\forall x_1 \ldots, x_n \cdot P$ is true if a value of $x_1 \ldots, x_n$ exists such that P is satisfied.

The types of all identifiers $x_1 \ldots, x_n$ must be inferable by P. They can be referenced in P.

Types The quantifiers and the P are predicates.

WD $\mathcal{L}(\forall x_1 \ldots, x_n \cdot P) \,\widehat{=}\, \forall x_1 \ldots, x_n \cdot \mathcal{L}(P)$
$\mathcal{L}(\exists x_1 \ldots, x_n \cdot P) \,\widehat{=}\, \forall x_1 \ldots, x_n \cdot \mathcal{L}(P)$

Equality

$$= \quad - \quad \texttt{=} \quad - \quad \text{equality}$$
$$\neq \quad - \quad \texttt{/=} \quad - \quad \text{inequality}$$

Description Checks if both expressions are or are not equal.

Definition $E \neq F \,\widehat{=}\, \neg(E = F)$

Types $E = F$ and $E \neq F$ are predicates with $E \in \alpha$ and $F \in \alpha$, i.e. E and F must have the same type.

WD $\mathcal{L}(E = F) \,\widehat{=}\, \mathcal{L}(E) \wedge \mathcal{L}(F)$
$\mathcal{L}(E \neq F) \,\widehat{=}\, \mathcal{L}(E) \wedge \mathcal{L}(F)$

Membership

$$\in \quad - \quad : \quad - \quad \text{set membership}$$
$$\notin \quad - \quad \texttt{/:} \quad - \quad \text{negated set membership}$$

Description Checks if an expression E denotes an element of a set S.

Definition $E \notin S \,\widehat{=}\, \neg(E \in S)$

Types $E \in S$ and $E \notin S$ are predicates with $E \in \alpha$ and $S \in \mathbb{P}(\alpha)$.

WD $\mathcal{L}(E \in S) \,\widehat{=}\, \mathcal{L}(E) \wedge \mathcal{L}(S)$
$\mathcal{L}(E \notin S) \,\widehat{=}\, \mathcal{L}(E) \wedge \mathcal{L}(S)$

3.3.3   Booleans

BOOL	—	BOOL	—	Boolean values
TRUE	—	TRUE	—	Boolean true
FALSE	—	FALSE	—	Boolean false
bool	—	bool	—	Convert a predicate into a Boolean value

Description BOOL is a pre-defined carrier set that contains the constants TRUE and FALSE.

bool(P) denotes the Boolean value of a predicate P. If P is true, the expression is TRUE. If P is false, the expression is FALSE.

Definition partition(BOOL, {TRUE}, {FALSE})
$$\text{bool(P)} = \text{TRUE} \Leftrightarrow \text{P}$$

Types $\text{BOOL} \in \mathbb{P}(\text{BOOL})$
$\text{TRUE} \in \text{BOOL}$
$\text{FALSE} \in \text{BOOL}$
$\text{bool(P)} \in \text{BOOL}$ with P being a predicate.

WD $\mathcal{L}(\text{BOOL}) \stackrel{\wedge}{=} \top$
$\mathcal{L}(\text{TRUE}) \stackrel{\wedge}{=} \top$
$\mathcal{L}(\text{FALSE}) \stackrel{\wedge}{=} \top$
$\mathcal{L}(\text{bool(P)}) \stackrel{\wedge}{=} \mathcal{L}(\text{P})$

3.3.4   Sets

Set comprehensions

{ ids · P $\mid$ E }	—	{ids.P|E}	—	Set comprehension
{ E $\mid$ P }	—	{E|P}	—	Set comprehension (short form)

Description *ids* is a comma-separated list of one ore more identifiers whose type must be inferable by the predicate P. The predicate P and E can contain references to the identifiers *ids*.

The set comprehension { $x_1, \ldots, x_n$ · P $\mid$ E } contains all values of E for the values of $x_1, \ldots, x_n$ where P is true.

{ E | P } is a short form for { *Free*(E) · P | E } where *Free*(E) denotes the list of free identifiers occurring in E (see Section 3.3.1)).

Definition { E | P } $\;\widehat{=}\;$ { *Free*(E) · P | E }

Types With $x_1 \in \alpha_1, \ldots, x_n \in \alpha_n$ and E $\in \beta$:
$$\{\, x_1, \ldots, x_n \cdot P \mid E \,\} \in \mathbb{P}(\beta)$$
$$\{\, E \mid P \,\} \in \mathbb{P}(\beta)$$

WD $\mathcal{L}(\{\, x_1, \ldots, x_n \cdot P \mid E \,\}) \quad \widehat{=} \quad \forall x_1, \ldots, x_n \cdot \mathcal{L}(P) \wedge (P \Rightarrow \mathcal{L}(E))$
$\mathcal{L}(\{\, E \mid P \,\}) \quad \widehat{=} \quad \forall \textit{Free}(E) \cdot \mathcal{L}(P) \wedge (P \Rightarrow \mathcal{L}(E))$

Example The following set comprehensions contain all the first 10 squares numbers:
$$\{1, 4, 9, 16, 25, 36, 49, 64, 81, 100\}$$
$$= \{\, x \cdot x \in 1 \mathinner{..} 10 \mid x \char`\^ 2 \,\}$$
$$= \{\, x \mid \exists y \cdot y \in 1 \mathinner{..} 10 \wedge x = y \char`\^ 2 \,\}$$
$$= \{\, x \char`\^ 2 \mid x \in 1 \mathinner{..} 10 \,\}$$

Basic sets

$\varnothing$	—	{}	— Empty set
{*exprs*}	—	{**exprs**}	— Set extension

Description *exprs* is a comma-separated list of one or more expressions of the same type.

The empty set $\varnothing$ contains no elements. The set extension $\{E_1, \ldots, E_n\}$ is the set that contains exactly the elements $E_1, \ldots, E_n$.

Definition $\varnothing \;\widehat{=}\; \{\, x \mid \bot \,\}$
$\{E_1, \ldots, E_n\} \;\widehat{=}\; \{\, x \mid x = E_1 \vee \ldots \vee x = E_n \,\}$

Types $\varnothing \in \mathbb{P}(\alpha)$, where α is an arbitrary type.
$\{E_1, \ldots, E_n\} \in \mathbb{P}(\alpha)$ with $E_1 \in \alpha, \ldots, E_n \in \alpha$

WD $\mathcal{L}(\varnothing) \;\widehat{=}\; \top$
$\mathcal{L}(\{E_1, \ldots, E_n\}) \;\widehat{=}\; \mathcal{L}(E_1) \wedge \ldots \wedge \mathcal{L}(E_n)$

Subsets

$$
\begin{array}{lll}
\subseteq & - \quad \texttt{<:} & - \quad \text{subset} \\
\not\subseteq & - \quad \texttt{/<:} & - \quad \text{not a subset} \\
\subset & - \quad \texttt{<<:} & - \quad \text{strict subset} \\
\not\subset & - \quad \texttt{/<<:} & - \quad \text{not a strict subset}
\end{array}
$$

Description $S \subseteq T$ checks if S is a subset of T, i.e. if all elements of S occur in T. $S \subset T$ checks if S is a subset of T and S does not equal T. $S \not\subseteq T$ and $S \not\subset T$ are the respective negated variants.

Definition $S \subseteq T \ \widehat{=}\ \forall e \cdot e \in S \Rightarrow e \in T$
$S \not\subseteq T \ \widehat{=}\ \neg (S \subseteq T)$
$S \subset T \ \widehat{=}\ S \subseteq T \wedge S \neq T$
$S \not\subset T \ \widehat{=}\ \neg (S \subset T)$

Types $S \square T$ is a predicate with $S \in \mathbb{P}(\alpha)$, $T \in \mathbb{P}(\alpha)$ for each operator $\square$ of $\subseteq$, $\not\subseteq$, $\subset$, $\not\subset$.

WD $\mathcal{L}(S \square T) \ \widehat{=}\ \mathcal{L}(S) \wedge \mathcal{L}(T)$ for each operator $\square$ of $\subseteq$, $\not\subseteq$, $\subset$, $\not\subset$.

Operations on sets

$$
\begin{array}{lll}
\cup & - \quad \backslash / & - \quad \text{Union} \\
\cap & - \quad / \backslash & - \quad \text{Intersection} \\
\backslash & - \quad \backslash & - \quad \text{Set subtraction}
\end{array}
$$

Description The union $S \cup T$ denotes the set that contains all elements that are in S or T. The intersection $S \cap T$ denotes the set that contains all elements that are in both S and T. The set subtraction or set difference $S \setminus T$ denotes all elements that are in S but not in T.

Definition $S \cup T \ \widehat{=}\ \{\, x \mid x \in S \vee x \in T \,\}$
$S \cap T \ \widehat{=}\ \{\, x \mid x \in S \wedge x \in T \,\}$
$S \setminus T \ \widehat{=}\ \{\, x \mid x \in S \wedge x \notin T \,\}$

Types $S \square T \in \mathbb{P}(\alpha)$ with $S \in \mathbb{P}(\alpha)$ and $T \in \mathbb{P}(\alpha)$ for each operator $\square$ of $\cup$, $\cap$, $\setminus$

WD $\mathcal{L}(S \square T) \ \widehat{=}\ \mathcal{L}(S) \wedge \mathcal{L}(T)$ for each operator $\square$ of $\cup$, $\cap$, $\setminus$

Power sets

$$\begin{array}{ccccc} \mathbb{P} & — & \texttt{POW} & — & \text{Power set} \\ \mathbb{P}_1 & — & \texttt{POW1} & — & \text{Set of non-empty subsets} \end{array}$$

Description $\mathbb{P}(S)$ denotes the set of all subsets of the set S. $\mathbb{P}(S)$ denotes the set of all non-empty subsets of the set S.

Definition $\mathbb{P}(S) \triangleq \{\, x \mid x \subseteq S \,\}$
$\mathbb{P}_1(S) \triangleq \mathbb{P}(S) \setminus \{\varnothing\}$

Types $\mathbb{P}(\alpha) \in \mathbb{P}(\mathbb{P}(\alpha))$ and $\mathbb{P}_1(\alpha) \in \mathbb{P}(\mathbb{P}(\alpha))$ with $S \in \mathbb{P}(\alpha)$.

WD $\mathcal{L}(\mathbb{P}(S)) \triangleq \mathcal{L}(S)$
$\mathcal{L}(\mathbb{P}_1(S)) \triangleq \mathcal{L}(S)$

Finite sets

$$\begin{array}{ccccc} \text{finite} & — & \texttt{finite} & — & \text{Finite set} \\ \text{card} & — & \texttt{card} & — & \text{Cardinality of a finite set} \end{array}$$

Description $\text{finite}(S)$ is a predicate that states that S is a finite set. $\text{card}(S)$ denotes the cardinality of S. The cardinality is only defined for finite sets.

Definition $\text{finite}(S) \triangleq \exists n, b \cdot n \in \mathbb{N} \wedge b \in S \rightarrowtail\!\!\!\!\rightarrow 1 .. n$
$\exists b \cdot b \in S \rightarrowtail\!\!\!\!\rightarrow 1 .. \text{card}(S)$

Types $\text{finite}(S)$ is a predicate and $\text{card}(S) \in \mathbb{Z}$ with $S \in \mathbb{P}(\alpha)$, i.e. S must be a set.

WD $\mathcal{L}(\text{finite}(S)) \triangleq \mathcal{L}(S)$
$\mathcal{L}(\text{card}(S)) \triangleq \mathcal{L}(S) \wedge \text{finite}(S)$

Partition

$$\begin{array}{ccccc} \text{partition} & — & \texttt{partition} & — & \text{Partitions of a set} \end{array}$$

Description $\text{partition}(S, s_1, \dots, s_n)$ is a predicate that states that the sets $s_1, \dots, s_n$ constitute a partition of S. The union of all elements of a partition is S and all elements are disjoint.

$\text{partition}(S)$ is equivalent to $S = \varnothing$ and $\text{partition}(S, s)$ to $S = s$.

Definition $\text{partition}(S, s_1, \dots, s_n) \triangleq S = s_1 \cup \dots \cup s_n \wedge \forall i, j \cdot i \neq j \Rightarrow s_i \cap s_j = \varnothing$

Types $\text{partition}(S, s_1, \dots, s_n)$ is a predicate with $S \in \mathbb{P}(\alpha)$ and $s_i \in \mathbb{P}(\alpha)$ for $i \in 1 .. n$

WD $\mathcal{L}(\text{partition}(S, s_1, \dots, s_n)) \triangleq \mathcal{L}(S) \wedge \mathcal{L}(s_1) \wedge \dots \wedge \mathcal{L}(s_n)$

Generalized union and intersection

union	— union —	Generalized union
inter	— inter —	Generalized intersection

Description union(S) is the union of all elements of S. inter(S) is the intersection of all elements of S. The intersection is only defined for non-empty S.

Definition $\text{union}(S) \; \widehat{=} \; \{ \; x \mid \exists s \cdot s \in S \wedge x \in s \; \}$
$\text{inter}(S) \; \widehat{=} \; \{ \; x \mid \forall s \cdot s \in S \Rightarrow x \in s \; \}$

Types $\text{union}(S) \in \mathbb{P}(\alpha)$ and $\text{inter}(S) \in \mathbb{P}(\alpha)$ with $S \in \mathbb{P}(\mathbb{P}(\alpha))$.

WD $\mathcal{L}(\text{union}(S)) \; \widehat{=} \; \mathcal{L}(S)$
$\mathcal{L}(\text{inter}(S)) \; \widehat{=} \; \mathcal{L}(S) \wedge S \neq \varnothing$

Quantified union and intersection

$\bigcup$	— UNION —	Quantified union
$\bigcap$	— INTER —	Quantified intersection

Description $\bigcup x_1 \ldots, x_n \cdot P \mid E$ is the union of all values of E for valuations of the identifiers $x_1 \ldots, x_n$ that fulfill the predicate P. The types of $x_1, \ldots, x_n$ must be inferable by P.

Analogously is $\bigcap x_1 \ldots, x_n \cdot P \mid E$ the intersection of all values of E for valuations of the identifiers $x_1 \ldots, x_n$ that fulfill the predicate P.

Like set comprehensions (3.3.4), the quantified union and intersection have a short form where the free variables of the expression are quantified implicitly: $\bigcup E \mid P$ and $\bigcap E \mid P$.

Definition $\bigcup x_1 \ldots, x_n \cdot P \mid E = \text{union}(\{ \; x_1 \ldots, x_n \cdot P \mid E\})$
$\bigcap x_1 \ldots, x_n \cdot P \mid E = \text{inter}(\{ \; x_1 \ldots, x_n \cdot P \mid E\})$
$\bigcup E \mid P = \bigcup \mathit{Free}(E) \cdot P \mid E$
$\bigcap E \mid P = \bigcap \mathit{Free}(E) \cdot P \mid E$

Types With $E \in \mathbb{P}(\alpha)$ and P being a predicate:
$(\bigcup x_1 \ldots, x_n \cdot P \mid E) \in \mathbb{P}(\alpha)$
$(\bigcap x_1 \ldots, x_n \cdot P \mid E) \in \mathbb{P}(\alpha)$
$(\bigcup E \mid P) \in \mathbb{P}(\alpha)$
$(\bigcap E \mid P) \in \mathbb{P}(\alpha)$

WD $\mathcal{L}(\bigcup x_1 \ldots, x_n \cdot P \mid E) \; \widehat{=} \; (\; \forall x_1 \ldots, x_n \cdot \mathcal{L}(P) \wedge (P \Rightarrow \mathcal{L}(E)) \;)$
$\mathcal{L}(\bigcap x_1 \ldots, x_n \cdot P \mid E) \; \widehat{=} \; (\; \forall x_1 \ldots, x_n \cdot \mathcal{L}(P) \wedge (P \Rightarrow \mathcal{L}(E)) \;) \wedge$
$\exists x_1 \ldots, x_n \cdot \mathcal{L}(P)$
$\mathcal{L}(\bigcup E \mid P) \; \widehat{=} \; (\; \forall \mathit{Free}(E) \cdot \mathcal{L}(P) \wedge (P \Rightarrow \mathcal{L}(E)) \;)$
$\mathcal{L}(\bigcap E \mid P) \; \widehat{=} \; (\; \forall \mathit{Free}(E) \cdot \mathcal{L}(P) \wedge (P \Rightarrow \mathcal{L}(E)) \;) \wedge \exists \mathit{Free}(E) \cdot \mathcal{L}(P)$

3.3.5 Relations

Pairs and Cartesian product

$\mapsto$	—	|->	—	Pair
$\times$	—	**	—	Cartesian product

Description $E \mapsto F$ denotes the pair whose first element is E and second element is F.

$S \times T$ denotes the set of pairs where the first element is a member of S and second element is a member of T.

Definition $S \times T \mathrel{\widehat{=}} \{\, x \mapsto y \mid x \in S \wedge y \in T \,\}$

Types $E \mapsto F \in \alpha \times \beta$ with $E \in \alpha$ and $F \in \beta$.
$S \times T \in \mathbb{P}(\alpha \times \beta)$ with $S \in \mathbb{P}(\alpha)$ and $T \in \mathbb{P}(\beta)$.

WD $\mathcal{L}(E \mapsto F) \mathrel{\widehat{=}} \mathcal{L}(E) \wedge \mathcal{L}(F)$
$\mathcal{L}(S \times T) \mathrel{\widehat{=}} \mathcal{L}(S) \wedge \mathcal{L}(T)$

Relations

$\leftrightarrow$	—	<->	—	Relations
$\leftrightarrow\!\!\!\leftarrow$	—	<<->	—	Total relations
$\leftrightarrow\!\!\!\rightarrow$	—	<->>	—	Surjective relations
$\leftrightarrow\!\!\!\leftrightarrow$	—	<<->>	—	Total surjective relations

Description $S \leftrightarrow T$ is the set of relations between the two sets S and T. A relation consists of pairs where the first element is of S and the second of T. $S \leftrightarrow T$ is just an abbreviation for $\mathbb{P}(S \times T)$.

A total relation is a relation which relates each element of S to at least one element of T.

A surjective relation is a relation where there is at least one element of S for each element of T such that both are related.

Definition $S \leftrightarrow T \mathrel{\widehat{=}} \mathbb{P}(S \times T)$
$S \mathbin{\leftarrow\!\!\!\leftrightarrow} T \mathrel{\widehat{=}} \{\, r \mid r \in S \leftrightarrow T \wedge \mathrm{dom}(r) = S \,\}$
$S \mathbin{\leftrightarrow\!\!\!\rightarrow} T \mathrel{\widehat{=}} \{\, r \mid r \in S \leftrightarrow T \wedge \mathrm{ran}(r) = T \,\}$
$S \mathbin{\leftrightarrow\!\!\!\leftrightarrow} T \mathrel{\widehat{=}} (S \mathbin{\leftarrow\!\!\!\leftrightarrow} T) \wedge (S \mathbin{\leftrightarrow\!\!\!\rightarrow} T)$

Types For $S \in \mathbb{P}(\alpha)$ and $T \in \mathbb{P}(\beta)$ for each operator $\square$ of $\leftrightarrow$, $\leftarrow\!\!\!\leftrightarrow$, $\leftrightarrow\!\!\!\rightarrow$, $\leftrightarrow\!\!\!\leftrightarrow$:
$S \square T \in \mathbb{P}(\mathbb{P}(\alpha \times \beta))$

WD $\mathcal{L}(S \square T) \mathrel{\widehat{=}} \mathcal{L}(S) \wedge \mathcal{L}(T)$ for each operator $\square$ of $\leftrightarrow$, $\leftarrow\!\!\!\leftrightarrow$, $\leftrightarrow\!\!\!\rightarrow$, $\leftrightarrow\!\!\!\leftrightarrow$.

Domain and Range

$$\text{dom} \quad - \quad \text{dom} \quad - \quad \text{Domain}$$
$$\text{ran} \quad - \quad \text{ran} \quad - \quad \text{Range}$$

Description If r is a relation between the sets S and T, the domain dom(r) is the set of the elements of S that are related to at least one element of T by r.

Likewise the range ran(r) is the set of elements of T to which at least one element of S relates by r.

Definition $\text{dom}(r) \mathrel{\widehat{=}} \{\, x \mid \exists y \cdot x \mapsto y \in r \,\}$
$\text{ran}(r) \mathrel{\widehat{=}} \{\, y \mid \exists x \cdot x \mapsto y \in r \,\}$

Types $\text{dom}(r) \in \mathbb{P}(\alpha)$ and $\text{ran}(r) \in \mathbb{P}(\beta)$ with $r \in \mathbb{P}(\alpha \times \beta)$.

WD $\mathcal{L}(\text{dom}(r)) \mathrel{\widehat{=}} \mathcal{L}(r)$
$\mathcal{L}(\text{ran}(r)) \mathrel{\widehat{=}} \mathcal{L}(r)$

Domain and Range Restrictions

◁	—	<|	—	Domain restriction
◄	—	<<|	—	Domain subtraction
▷	—	|>	—	Range restriction
▶	—	|>>	—	Range subtraction

Description The domain restriction $S \triangleleft r$ is a subset of the relation r that contains all of the pairs whose first element is in S. $S \blacktriangleleft r$ is the subset where the pair's first element is *not* in S.

In the same way, the range restriction $r \triangleright S$ is a subset that contains all of the pairs whose second element is in S and $r \blacktriangleright S$ is the set where the pair's second element is not in S.

Definition $S \triangleleft r \mathrel{\widehat{=}} \{\, x \mapsto y \mid x \mapsto y \in r \wedge x \in S\}$
$S \blacktriangleleft r \mathrel{\widehat{=}} \{\, x \mapsto y \mid x \mapsto y \in r \wedge x \notin S\}$
$r \triangleright S \mathrel{\widehat{=}} \{\, x \mapsto y \mid x \mapsto y \in r \wedge y \in S\}$
$r \blacktriangleright S \mathrel{\widehat{=}} \{\, x \mapsto y \mid x \mapsto y \in r \wedge y \notin S\}$

Types $S \triangleleft r \in \mathbb{P}(\alpha \times \beta)$ and $S \blacktriangleleft r \in \mathbb{P}(\alpha \times \beta)$ with $r \in \mathbb{P}(\alpha \times \beta)$ and $S \in \mathbb{P}(\alpha)$
$r \triangleright S \in \mathbb{P}(\alpha \times \beta)$ and $r \blacktriangleright S \in \mathbb{P}(\alpha \times \beta)$ with $r \in \mathbb{P}(\alpha \times \beta)$ and $S \in \mathbb{P}(\beta)$

WD $\mathcal{L}(S \mathbin{\square} r) \mathrel{\widehat{=}} \mathcal{L}(S) \wedge \mathcal{L}(r)$ for each operator $\square$ of ◁, ◄, ▷, ▶

Operations on relations

;	—	;	—	Relational forward composition
∘	—	circ	—	Relational backward composition
⩤	—	<+	—	Relational override
∥	—	||	—	Parallel product
⊗	—	><	—	Direct product
$^{-1}$	—	~	—	Inverse

Description An element x is related by r ; S to an element y if there is an element z such that r relates x to z and S relates z to y.

s ∘ r can be written as an alternative to r ; s. This reflects the fact that $f(g(x)) = (f \circ g)(x)$ holds for two functions f and g.

The relational overwrite r ⩤ s is equal to r except all entries in r whose first element is in the domain of s are replaced by the corresponding entries in s.

The parallel product r ∥ s relates a pair $x \mapsto y$ to a pair $m \mapsto n$ when r relates x to m and s relates y to n.

If a relation r relates an element x to y and s relates x to z, the direct product r ⊗ s relates x to the pair $y \mapsto z$.

The inverse relation r^{-1} relates an element x to y if the original relation r relates y to x.

Definition r ; s $\mathrel{\widehat{=}}$ { $x \mapsto y \mid \exists z \cdot x \mapsto z \in r \land z \mapsto y \in s$ }
r ∘ s $\mathrel{\widehat{=}}$ s ; r
r ⩤ s $\mathrel{\widehat{=}}$ s ∪ $(dom(s) \lhd r)$
r ∥ s $\mathrel{\widehat{=}}$ { $(x \mapsto y) \mapsto (m \mapsto n) \mid x \mapsto m \in r \land y \mapsto n \in s$ }
r ⊗ s $\mathrel{\widehat{=}}$ { $x \mapsto (y \mapsto z) \mid x \mapsto y \in r \land x \mapsto z \in s$ }
$r^{-1} \mathrel{\widehat{=}}$ { $y \mapsto x \mid x \mapsto y \in r$ }

Types r ; s $\in \mathbb{P}(\alpha \times \gamma)$ with r $\in \mathbb{P}(\alpha \times \beta)$ and s $\in \mathbb{P}(\beta \times \gamma)$
r ∘ s $\in \mathbb{P}(\gamma \times \alpha)$ with r $\in \mathbb{P}(\alpha \times \beta)$ and s $\in \mathbb{P}(\beta \times \gamma)$
r ⩤ s $\in \mathbb{P}(\alpha \times \beta)$ with r $\in \mathbb{P}(\alpha \times \beta)$ and s $\in \mathbb{P}(\alpha \times \beta)$
r ∥ s $\in \mathbb{P}(\,(\alpha \times \gamma) \times (\beta \times \delta)\,)$ with r $\in \mathbb{P}(\alpha \times \beta)$ and s $\in \mathbb{P}(\gamma \times \delta)$
r ⊗ s $\in \mathbb{P}(\alpha \times (\beta \times \gamma))$ with r $\in \mathbb{P}(\alpha \times \beta)$ and s $\in \mathbb{P}(\alpha \times \gamma)$
$r^{-1} \in \mathbb{P}(\beta \times \alpha)$ with r $\in \mathbb{P}(\alpha \times \beta)$

WD $\mathcal{L}(r \,\square\, s) \mathrel{\widehat{=}} \mathcal{L}(r) \land \mathcal{L}(s)$ for each operator $\square$ of ;, ∘, ⩤, ∥, ⊗
$\mathcal{L}(r^{-1}) \mathrel{\widehat{=}} \mathcal{L}(r)$

Relational image

$$[\ldots] \quad - \quad [\ldots] \quad - \quad \text{Relational image}$$

Description The relational image r[S] are those elements in the range of r that are mapped from S.

Definition $r[S] \mathrel{\widehat{=}} \{\, y \mid \exists x \cdot x \in S \wedge x \mapsto y \in r \,\}$

Types $r[S] \in \mathbb{P}(\beta)$ with $r \in \mathbb{P}(\alpha \times \beta)$ and $S \in \mathbb{P}(\alpha)$

WD $\mathcal{L}(r[S]) \mathrel{\widehat{=}} \mathcal{L}(r) \wedge \mathcal{L}(S)$

Constant relations

id	—	`id`	—	Identity relation
prj_1	—	`prj1`	—	First projection
prj_2	—	`prj2`	—	Second projection

Description id is the identity relation that maps every element to itself.

prj_1 is a function that maps a pair to its first element. Likewise prj_2 maps a pair to its second element.

id, prj_1 and prj_2 are generic definitions. Their type must be inferred from the environment.

Definition $\text{id} \mathrel{\widehat{=}} \{\, x \mapsto x \mid \top \,\}$
$\text{prj}_1 \mathrel{\widehat{=}} \{\, (x \mapsto y) \mapsto x \mid \top \,\}$
$\text{prj}_2 \mathrel{\widehat{=}} \{\, (x \mapsto y) \mapsto y \mid \top \,\}$

Types $\text{id} \in \mathbb{P}(\alpha \times \alpha)$ for an arbitrary type α.
$\text{prj}_1 \in \mathbb{P}((\alpha \times \beta) \times \alpha)$ and $\text{prj}_1 \in \mathbb{P}((\alpha \times \beta) \times \beta)$ for arbitrary types α and β.

WD $\mathcal{L}(\text{id}) \mathrel{\widehat{=}} \top$
$\mathcal{L}(\text{prj}_1) \mathrel{\widehat{=}} \top$
$\mathcal{L}(\text{prj}_2) \mathrel{\widehat{=}} \top$

Example The assumption that a relation r is irreflexive can be expressed by:
$r \cap \text{id} = \varnothing$

Sets of functions

$\rightarrow\!\!\!+$	—	+->	—	Partial functions
$\rightarrow$	—	-->	—	Total functions
$\rightarrowtail\!\!+$	—	>+>	—	Partial injections
$\rightarrowtail$	—	>->	—	Total injections
$\twoheadrightarrow\!\!+$	—	+->>	—	Partial surjections
$\twoheadrightarrow$	—	-->>	—	Total surjections
$\rightarrowtail\!\!\!\!\twoheadrightarrow$	—	>->>	—	Bijections

Description A partial function from S to T is a relation that maps an element of S to at most one element of T. A function is total if its domain contains all elements of S, i.e. it maps every element of S to an element of T.

A function is injective (is an injection) if two distinct elements of S are always mapped to distinct elements of T. It is also equivalent to say that the inverse of an injective function is a also a function.

A function is surjective (is a surjection) if for every element of T there exists an element in S that is mapped to it.

A function is bijective (is a bijection) if it is both injective and surjective.

Definition $S \nrightarrow T \mathrel{\widehat{=}} \{\, f \mid f \in S \leftrightarrow T \wedge (\forall e, x, y \cdot e \mapsto x \in f \wedge e \mapsto y \in f \Rightarrow x = y)\,\}$
$S \rightarrow T \mathrel{\widehat{=}} \{\, f \mid f \in S \nrightarrow T \wedge \mathrm{dom}(f) = S\,\}$
$S \rightarrowtail\!\!\!+ T \mathrel{\widehat{=}} \{\, f \mid f \in S \nrightarrow T \wedge f^{-1} \in T \nrightarrow S\,\}$
$S \rightarrowtail T \mathrel{\widehat{=}} (S \rightarrowtail\!\!\!+ T) \cap (S \rightarrow T)$
$S \twoheadrightarrow\!\!+ T \mathrel{\widehat{=}} \{\, f \mid f \in S \nrightarrow T \wedge \mathrm{ran}(f) = T\,\}$
$S \twoheadrightarrow T \mathrel{\widehat{=}} (S \twoheadrightarrow\!\!+ T) \cap (S \rightarrow T)$
$S \rightarrowtail\!\!\!\!\twoheadrightarrow T \mathrel{\widehat{=}} (S \rightarrowtail T) \cap (S \twoheadrightarrow T)$

Types $S \in \mathbb{P}(\alpha)$, $T \in \mathbb{P}(\beta)$ for each operator $\square$ of $\nrightarrow$, $\rightarrow$, $\rightarrowtail\!\!+$, $\rightarrowtail$, $\twoheadrightarrow\!\!+$, $\twoheadrightarrow$, $\rightarrowtail\!\!\!\!\twoheadrightarrow$:
$S \mathbin{\square} T \in \mathbb{P}(\mathbb{P}(\alpha \times \beta))$

WD For each operator $\square$ of $\nrightarrow$, $\rightarrow$, $\rightarrowtail\!\!+$, $\rightarrowtail$, $\twoheadrightarrow\!\!+$, $\twoheadrightarrow$, $\rightarrowtail\!\!\!\!\twoheadrightarrow$:
$\mathcal{L}(S \mathbin{\square} T) \mathrel{\widehat{=}} \mathcal{L}(S) \wedge \mathcal{L}(T)$

Function application

$$(\ldots) \quad - \quad (\ldots) \quad - \quad \text{Function application}$$

Description The function application f(a) yields the value for a of the function f. It is only defined if a is in the domain of f and if f is actually a function.

Definition $a \mapsto f(a) \in f$

Types $f(a) \in \beta$ with $f \in \mathbb{P}(\alpha \times \beta)$ and $a \in \alpha$

WD $\mathcal{L}(f(a)) \cong \mathcal{L}(f) \wedge \mathcal{L}(a) \wedge f \in \alpha \nrightarrow \beta \wedge a \in \text{dom}(f)$ with $\mathbb{P}(\alpha \times \beta)$ being the type of f.

Lambda

$$\lambda \quad - \quad \% \quad - \quad \text{Lambda}$$

Description $(\lambda\, p \cdot P \mid E\,)$ is a function that maps an "input" p to a result E such that P holds.

p is a pattern of identifiers, parentheses and $\mapsto$ which follows the following rules:

- An identifier x is a pattern.
- An identifier x, followed by an $\overset{\circ}{\circ}$ operator is a pattern (See 3.3.7 for more details).
- A pair $a \mapsto b$ is a pattern if a and b are patterns.
- (a) is pattern if a is pattern.

In the simplest case, p is just an identifier.

Definition $(\lambda\, p \cdot P \mid E\,) \cong \{\, p \mapsto E \mid P\,\}$

Types $(\lambda\, p \cdot P \mid E\,) \in \mathbb{P}(\,\alpha \times \beta\,)$ with $p \in \alpha$, P being a predicate and $E \in \beta$.

WD $\mathcal{L}(\lambda\, p \cdot P \mid E\,) \cong \forall Free(p) \cdot \mathcal{L}(P) \wedge (P \Rightarrow \mathcal{L}(E))$

Example A function *double* that returns the double value of a natural number:
$double = (\lambda x \cdot x \in \mathbb{N} \mid 2 \cdot x)$

The dot product of two 2-dimensional vectors can be defined by:
$dotp = (\lambda\, (a \mapsto b) \mapsto (c \mapsto d) \cdot a \in \mathbb{Z} \wedge b \in \mathbb{Z} \wedge c \in \mathbb{Z} \wedge d \in \mathbb{Z} \mid a \cdot c + b \cdot d\,)$

3.3.6 Arithmetic

Sets of numbers

$\mathbb{Z}$	—	INT	—	Integers
$\mathbb{N}$	—	NAT	—	Natural numbers, starting with 0
$\mathbb{N}_1$	—	NAT1	—	Natural numbers, starting with 1
..	—	..	—	Range of numbers

Description The set of all integers is denoted by $\mathbb{Z}$. It contains all elements of the type. The two subsets $\mathbb{N}$ and $\mathbb{N}_1$ contain all elements greater than or equal to 0 and 1 respectively. The range of numbers between a and b is denoted by a .. b.

Definition $\mathbb{N} \mathrel{\hat{=}} \{\, n \mid n \in \mathbb{Z} \land n \geq 0 \,\}$
$\mathbb{N}_1 \mathrel{\hat{=}} \{\, n \mid n \in \mathbb{Z} \land n \geq 1 \,\}$
$\mathsf{a} .. \mathsf{b} \mathrel{\hat{=}} \{\, n \mid n \in \mathbb{Z} \land \mathsf{a} \leq n \land n \leq \mathsf{b} \,\}$

Types $\mathbb{Z} \in \mathbb{P}(\mathbb{Z})$
$\mathbb{N} \in \mathbb{P}(\mathbb{Z})$
$\mathbb{N}_1 \in \mathbb{P}(\mathbb{Z})$
$\mathsf{a} .. \mathsf{b} \in \mathbb{P}(\mathbb{Z})$ with $\mathsf{a} \in \mathbb{Z}$ and $\mathsf{b} \in \mathbb{Z}$

WD $\mathcal{L}(\mathbb{Z}) \mathrel{\hat{=}} \top$
$\mathcal{L}(\mathbb{N}) \mathrel{\hat{=}} \top$
$\mathcal{L}(\mathbb{N}_1) \mathrel{\hat{=}} \top$
$\mathcal{L}(\mathsf{a} .. \mathsf{b}) \mathrel{\hat{=}} \mathcal{L}(\mathsf{a}) \land \mathcal{L}(\mathsf{b})$

Arithmetic operations

$+$	—	+	—	Addition
$-$	—	-	—	Subtraction or unary minus
$\cdot$	—	*	—	Multiplication
$\div$	—	/	—	Integer division
mod	—	mod	—	Modulo
$\char`\^$	—	^	—	Exponentiation

Description These are the usual arithmetic operations.

Definition Addition, subtraction and multiplication behave as expected.

The division is defined in a way that $1 \div 2 = 0$ and $-1 \div 2 = 0$:
$\mathsf{a} \div \mathsf{b} = \max(\{\, c \mid c \in \mathbb{N} \land \mathsf{b} \cdot c \leq \mathsf{a} \,\})$ for $\mathsf{a} \in \mathbb{N}$ and $\mathsf{b} \in \mathbb{N}$
$(-a) \div b = -(a \div b)$
$a \div (-b) = -(a \div b)$

$$\text{a mod b} = c \;\widehat{=}\; c \in 0 \mathinner{.\,.} b - 1 \wedge \exists k \cdot k \in \mathbb{N} \wedge k \cdot b + c = a$$

Types With a $\in \mathbb{Z}$, b $\in \mathbb{Z}$ for each operator $\square$ of $+$, $-$, $\cdot$, $\div$, mod:
$$\text{a} \,\square\, \text{b} \in \mathbb{Z}$$
$$-\text{a} \in \mathbb{Z}$$

WD $\mathcal{L}(\text{a} + \text{b}) \,\widehat{=}\, \mathcal{L}(\text{a}) \wedge \mathcal{L}(\text{b})$
$\mathcal{L}(\text{a} - \text{b}) \,\widehat{=}\, \mathcal{L}(\text{a}) \wedge \mathcal{L}(\text{b})$
$\mathcal{L}(-\text{a}) \,\widehat{=}\, \mathcal{L}(\text{a})$
$\mathcal{L}(\text{a} \cdot \text{b}) \,\widehat{=}\, \mathcal{L}(\text{a}) \wedge \mathcal{L}(\text{b})$
$\mathcal{L}(\text{a} \div \text{b}) \,\widehat{=}\, \mathcal{L}(\text{a}) \wedge \mathcal{L}(\text{b}) \wedge \text{b} \neq 0$
$\mathcal{L}(\text{a} \bmod \text{b}) \,\widehat{=}\, \mathcal{L}(\text{a}) \wedge \mathcal{L}(\text{b}) \wedge \text{a} \geq 0 \wedge \text{b} > 0$
$\mathcal{L}(\text{a} \,\widehat{}\, \text{b}) \,\widehat{=}\, \mathcal{L}(\text{a}) \wedge \mathcal{L}(\text{b}) \wedge \text{a} \geq 0 \wedge \text{b} \geq 0$

Minimum and Maximum

min	—	**min**	— Minimum
max	—	**max**	— Maximum

Description min(S) and max(S) denotes the smallest and largest number in the set of integers S respectively.

The minimum and maximum are only defined if such a number exists.

Definition $\min(\text{S}) \in \text{S} \wedge (\forall x \cdot x \in \text{S} \Rightarrow \min(\text{S}) \leq x)$
$\max(\text{S}) \in \text{S} \wedge (\forall x \cdot x \in \text{S} \Rightarrow \max(\text{S}) \geq x)$

Types $\min(\text{S}) \in \mathbb{Z}$ and $\max(\text{S}) \in \mathbb{Z}$ with $\text{S} \in \mathbb{P}(\mathbb{Z})$.

WD $\mathcal{L}(\min(\text{S})) \,\widehat{=}\, \mathcal{L}(\text{S}) \wedge \text{S} \neq \varnothing \wedge \exists b \cdot \forall x \cdot x \in \text{S} \Rightarrow b \leq x$
$\mathcal{L}(\max(\text{S})) \,\widehat{=}\, \mathcal{L}(\text{S}) \wedge \text{S} \neq \varnothing \wedge \exists b \cdot \forall x \cdot x \in \text{S} \Rightarrow b \geq x$

3.3.7 Typing

$\overset{\circ}{\circ}$	—	**oftype**	— of type

Description $\text{E} \overset{\circ}{\circ} \alpha$ is an expression that has exactly the value of E but its type is specified by the type expression α (3.3.1).

E is restricted to expressions whose type does not depend on an argument of that expression. These are the constant relations id, prj_1, prj_2 and the empty set $\varnothing$.

Another location where the operator can be used is the declaration of bound variables in quantifiers and patterns in lambda expressions. Each identifier can be followed by $\mathbin{⦂}$ and the identifier's type.

Definition $\mathsf{E} \mathbin{⦂} \alpha = \mathsf{E}$

> **Types** $\mathsf{E} \mathbin{⦂} \alpha \in \alpha$ with $\mathsf{E} \in \alpha$

> **WD** $\mathcal{L}(\mathsf{E} \mathbin{⦂} \alpha) \mathrel{\widehat{=}} \mathcal{L}(\mathsf{E})$

Example The predicate $\varnothing = \varnothing$ is not correctly typed in Event-B because the types of $\varnothing$ are not inferable. A valid alternative would be:
$$(\varnothing \mathbin{⦂} \mathbb{Z}) = \varnothing$$

The predicate $\exists x, y \cdot x \neq y$ is not correctly typed because the types of x and y cannot be inferred: A valid alternative (for integers) is:
$$\exists x \mathbin{⦂} \mathbb{Z}, y \cdot x \neq y$$

The following lambda expression uses the $\mathbin{⦂}$ operator:
$$(\lambda x \mathbin{⦂} \mathbb{Z} \mapsto y \mathbin{⦂} \mathrm{BOOL} \mid x > 0 \cdot x + 1)$$
An arguably more readable version without the use of $\mathbin{⦂}$ is:
$$(\lambda x \mapsto y \mid x > 0 \wedge y \in \mathrm{BOOL} \cdot x + 1)$$

3.3.8 Assignments

Deterministic Assignments

$$:= \quad — \quad := \quad — \quad \text{deterministic assignment}$$

Description $x_1, \ldots, x_n := \mathsf{E}_1 \ldots, \mathsf{E}_n$ assigns the expressions E_i to the variable x_i, with $i \in 1..n$. All x_i must be distinct identifiers that refer to variables of the concrete machine.

There is a special form of the assignment which uses a relational overwrite:
$$x(\mathsf{F}) := \mathsf{E}.$$

Definition The before-after-predicate of $x_1, \ldots, x_n := \mathsf{E}_1, \ldots, \mathsf{E}_n$ is
$$x_1' = \mathsf{E}_1 \wedge \ldots \wedge x_n' = \mathsf{E}_n.$$

This assignment is equivalent to $x_1, \ldots, x_n :\mid x_1' = \mathsf{E}_1 \wedge \ldots \wedge x_n' = \mathsf{E}_n$.

The special form for this assignment is:

$$x(F) := E \quad \hat{=} \quad x := x \Leftarrow \{\, F \mapsto E \,\}$$

Types x_i and E_i must have the same type: $x_i \in \alpha_i$ and $E_i \in \alpha_i$ for $i \in 1\mathinner{\ldotp\ldotp} n$.

WD $\mathcal{L}(\, x_1, \ldots, x_n := E_1, \ldots, E_n \,) \quad \hat{=} \quad \mathcal{L}(E_1) \wedge \ldots \wedge \mathcal{L}(E_n)$
$\mathcal{L}(\, x(F) := E \,) \quad \hat{=} \quad \mathcal{L}(F) \wedge \mathcal{L}(E)$

Non-deterministic assignment with before-after-predicate

:| —   :| —   non-deterministic assignment with a before-after-predicate

Description $x_1, \ldots, x_n :|\ Q$ assigns any value to the variables $x_1 \ldots, x_n$ such that the the before-after-predicate Q is fulfilled. Each x_i is an identifier that refers to a variable of the concrete machine.

All free identifiers in Q must be constants, concrete parameters, concrete variables or primed versions of the modified variables $(x'_1, \ldots, x'_n)$.

This is the most general form of assignment. All other assignments can be converted to this.

Definition The before-after-predicate is Q.

Types Q is a predicate and all x_i and x'_i must have the same type: $x_1 \in \alpha_i$ and $x'_1 \in \alpha_i$ for $i \in 1\mathinner{\ldotp\ldotp} n$.

WD $\mathcal{L}(\, x_1, \ldots, x_n :|\ Q \,) \quad \hat{=} \quad \forall x'_1, \ldots, x'_n \cdot \mathcal{L}(\, Q \,)$

Feasibility $\mathcal{F}(\, x_1, \ldots, x_n :|\ Q(x'_1, \ldots, x'_n) \,)$
$\hat{=} \quad \exists x'_1, \ldots, x'_n \cdot Q(x'_1, \ldots, x'_n)$

Non-deterministic assignment by sets

:∈   —   ::   —   non-deterministic assignment of a set member

Description $x :\in E$ assigns any value of the set E to the variable x. x is an identifier that refers to a variable of the concrete machine.

All free identifiers in E must be constants, concrete variables or concrete parameters.

Definition The before-after-predicate is $x' \in E$.
The assignment is equivalent to $x :\mid x' \in E$.

Types $x \in \alpha$ and $E \in \mathbb{P}(\alpha)$

WD $\mathcal{L}(\ x :\in E\ ) \quad \widehat{=} \quad \mathcal{L}(E)$

Feasibility $\mathcal{F}(\ x :\in E\ ) \quad \widehat{=} \quad E \neq \varnothing$

3.4   Proving

In Section 3.2.7, we learned what proof obligations are generated by Rodin from an Event-B model. We validate the model by discharging proof obligations. This is what we call proving.

 In this chapter we will:

- Explain proof rules
- Explain tactics
- Explain and describe provers
- Explain reasoners
- Describe how to perform automatic and manual proving
- Purge proofs for maintenance
- Simplify proofs for maintainability and storage

3.4.1   Sequents

A sequent is a formal statement describing something we want to prove.

Sequents are of the following form

$H \vdash G$

where H is the set of hypotheses (predicates) and G is the goal that can be proved from the predicates.

The above statement can be read as follows: Under the hypotheses H, prove the goal G.

3.4.2   Proof Rules

In its pure mathematical form, a proof rule is a tool to perform a formal proof and is denoted by:

$$\frac{A}{C}$$

where A is a (possibly empty) list of sequents (the antecedents of the proof rule) and C is a sequent (the consequent of the rule). We interpret the above proof rule as follows: The combination of the proofs of each sequent of A prove the sequent C.

 Example: Consider the following proof rule:

$$\frac{E_1}{E_1 \vee E_2}$$

This says that if E_1 is valid, then the statement $E_1 \vee E_2$ must be valid as well. Thus, we can replace the sequent by the consequent.

Proof Rule Representation in Rodin

In Rodin, the representation for proof rules is more structured not only to reduce the space required to store the rule but, more importantly, to support proof reuse. A proof rule in Rodin contains the following:

used goal A used goal predicate.

used hypotheses The set of used hypotheses.

antecedents A list of antecedents (to be explained later).

reasoner The reasoner used to generate this proof rule (see Section 3.4.6).

reasoner input The input for the reasoner to generate this proof rule (reasoners are explained in Section 3.4.6).

Each antecedent of the proof rule contains the following information:

new goal A new goal predicate.

added hypotheses The set of added hypotheses.

With this representation, a proof rule in Rodin corresponding to a proof schema as follows:

$$\frac{H, H_u, H_{A_0} \vdash G_{A_0} \quad \ldots \quad H, H_u, H_{A_n-1} \vdash G_{A_n-1}}{H, H_u \vdash G_u}$$

Where:

- H_u is the set of used hypotheses

- G_u is the used goal

- H_{A_i} is the set of added hypotheses corresponding to the ith antecedent.

- G_{A_i} is the new goal corresponding to the ith antecedent.

- H is the meta-variable that can be instantiated.

Applying Proof Rules

Given a proof rule of the form mentioned above, the following describes how to apply this rule to an input sequent. If the process is successful, a list of output sequences is produced.

- The rule is not applicable if the goal of the sequent is not exactly the same as the used goal or if any of the used hypotheses are not contained in the set of hypotheses of the input sequent.

- If the rule is applicable, the antecedent sequents are returned. The goal of each antecedent sequent is the new goal. The hypotheses of each antecedent sequent are the union of the old hypotheses and added hypotheses of the corresponding antecedent.

 The user interface for proving is explained in Section 3.1.7. The practical application of proof rules is explained in Section 2.9.6.

3.4.3   Proof Tactics

Tactics provide an easier way to construct and manage proof search and manipulation. They provide calls to the underlying reasoners or other tactics to modify proofs.

 A list of all proof tactics is maintained in the Rodin Wiki.[4] This list is very comprehensive — be sure to check it out!

Tactics can be applied as follows:

Automatic Rodin can automatically apply a number of tactics after each manual proof step.

Proof tree Pruning the proof tree is a tactic that can be applied from the proof tree through the context menu. Other tactics may be available there.

In sequents Some sequents have elements that are highlighted in red. Clicking on these elements brings up a menu with all applicable tactics so that they can be applied manually.

It may be useful to consider the following categories of tactics:

Basic Tactics

Basic tactics are tactics that change the proof tree only at the point of application.

- Prune - This tactic is a direct application of the pruning facility providing by the proof tree. The tactic is successful if the input node is not pending.

- Rule Application Tactics - Tactics of this class provide a wrapper around a proof rule (3.4.2). The tactic is successful if the proof rule is successfully applied to the input node.

- Reasoner Application Tactics - Tactics of this class provide a wrapper around a reasoner (3.4.6). The tactic is successful if the reasoner is successfully applied to the input node.

---

[4]http://wiki.event-b.org/index.php/Rodin_Proof_Tactics

Tactical Tactics

Tactical tactics are constructed from existing tactics. They indicate different strategic or heuristic decisions.

- Apply on All Pending - A tactic to apply a specific sub-tactic to all pending nodes at the point of application. The tactic is successful if the sub-tactic is successful on one of the pending nodes.

- Repeating - A tactic that repeats a specific sub-tactic at the point of application until it fails. The tactic is successful if a sub-tactic is successful at least once.

- Composing Sequential - A tactic to compose a list of sub-tactics that can be applied to the point of application. The tactic is successful if one of the sub-tactics is successful.

More complex proof strategy can be constructed by combining the above tactical tactics.

3.4.4 Provers

In the end, provers perform the actual work. Rodin comes with one prover installed (New PP). It is strongly recommended that you install the third-party provers from Atelier B (as described in Section 3.4.4) in order to add the PP and ML provers. More provers may be available as plugins.

We will now give a very brief overview of the existing provers by pointing out their strengths/weaknesses.

PP

We recommend trying the PP prover first because it is sound and does a pretty good job.

Names in the proof control: P0, P1, PP

Names in the proof tree: PP

Names in the preferences: Atelier B P0, Atelier B P1, Atelier B PP

Input: In the configuration "P0", all selected hypotheses and the goal are passed to PP. In the configuration "P1", one lasso operation is applied to the selected hypotheses and the goal and the result is passed to PP. In the configuration "PP", all the available hypotheses are passed to PP.

How the Prover Proceeds: The input sequent is translated to classical B and fed to the PP prover of Atelier B. PP works in a manner similar to newPP but with support for equational and arithmetic reasoning.

Some Strengths:

- PP has limited support for equational and arithmetic reasoning.

Some Weaknesses:

- PP does not output a set of used hypotheses.
- PP is unaware of some set theoretical axioms.
- PP has similar problems to New PP with regard to well-definedness.
- If unnecessary hypotheses are present, they may prevent PP from finding a proof even when the proof obligation obviously holds.

ML

The ML prover can be quite helpful when the proofs involve arithmetic.

Names in the proof control: M0, M1, M2, M3, ML

Names in the proof tree: ML

Names in the preferences: Atelier B ML

Input: All visible hypotheses are passed to ML. The different configurations refer to the configuration (proof force) of the ML prover.

How the Prover Proceeds: ML applies a mix of forward, backward and rewriting rules in order to discharge the goal (or detect a contradiction among hypotheses).

Some Strengths:

- ML has limited support for equational and arithmetic reasoning.
- ML is more resilient to unnecessary hypotheses than newPP and PP.

Some Weaknesses:

- ML does not output a set of used hypotheses.
- Not all set theoretical axioms are part of ML.

New PP

 New PP is unsound. There have been several bug reports. Some have been fixed, but at this point we do not recommend New PP for inexperienced users.

Names in the proof control: nPP R., nPP with a lasso symbol, nPP

Names in the proof tree: Predicate Prover

Names in the preferences: PP restricted, PP after lasso, PP unrestricted

Input: In the configuration "restricted", all selected hypotheses and the goal are passed to New PP. In the configuration "after lasso", a lasso operation is applied to the selected hypotheses and the goal and the result is passed to New PP. The lasso operation selects any unselected hypothesis that have a common symbol with the goal or a hypothesis that is currently selected. In the configuration "unrestricted", all the available hypotheses are passed to New PP.

How the Prover Proceeds: First, all function and predicate symbols that are different from "$\in$" and not related to arithmetic are translated away. For example $A \subseteq B$ is translated to $\forall x \cdot x \in A \Rightarrow x \in B$. Then New PP translates the proof obligation to CNF (conjunctive normal form) and applies a combination of unit resolution and the Davis Putnam algorithm.

Some Strengths:

- New PP outputs a set of "used hypotheses". If an unused hypotheses changes, the old proof can be reused.

- New PP has limited support for equational reasoning.

Some Weaknesses:

- New PP is unsound. There have been several bug reports.

- New PP does not support arithmetic; hence, $\vdash_{\mathcal{L}} 1 = 1$ is discharged, but $\vdash_{\mathcal{L}} 1 + 1 = 2$ is not. Note that arithmetic reasoning when the formula is not ground (i.e. the formula contains variables) is a long standing challenge.

- New PP is unaware of set theoretical axioms. In particular, $\vdash_{\mathcal{L}} \exists A \cdot \forall x \cdot x \in A \Leftrightarrow x \in B \lor x \in C$ is not recognized because the union axiom is not available within New PP. This means that New PP can only reuse sets that already appear in the formula, but it is unable to introduce new sets. Note that set theoretical reasoning is perceived as a hard problem.

- If unnecessary hypotheses are present, they may prevent New PP from finding a proof even when the proof obligation obviously holds. We therefore advise you to unselect unnecessary hypotheses.

- New PP does not take well-definedness into account: Lemma $\vdash_{\mathcal{L}} b \in f^{-1}[\{f(b)\}]$ is not discharged. In fact, this sequent has exactly the same translation as $\vdash_{\mathcal{L}} b \in \mathrm{dom}(f)$, which cannot be proved.

- New PP tends to run out of memory if the input is large.

3.4.5 How to Use the Provers Effectively

It is very hard, in general, to predict whether a certain automatic prover can or cannot discharge a given proof obligation within a given amount of time. (This is also the case for many other automatic first order theorem provers.)

Therefore applying the 11 configurations in a trial and error fashion is often frustrating.

The following guidelines may be useful:

- Add PP restricted, P0, and ML to the auto-tactic. If the auto-tactic runs out of memory, remove PP.

- If the model is small, add PP after lasso and P1 to the auto-tactic.

- Whenever you think that the current proof obligation should be discharged automatically, invoke the auto-tactic (⚙) instead of some particular automatic prover.

- If the auto-tactic fails, it is usually best to simplify the proof obligation in some way. The most important ways of simplifying the proof obligation are:

  - Remove unnecessary hypotheses; add required hypotheses that have been missing.

  - Create a case distinction

  - Instantiate quantifiers.

  - Apply ae (abstract expression) to replace complicated expressions with fresh variables.

- You can also apply one of the automatic provers. They may be more successful than the auto-tactic because they have a longer timeout.

  - The configurations that act on more than the selected hypotheses (unrestricted P1, PP and ML) become useless when the model grows.

- When everything fails, try to solve the proof obligation manually by clicking on the red symbols.

  - You may discover that some assumption was missing.

  - You may complete the proof.

  - If you observe that a valid proof obligation cannot be proved manually, please send a bug report (4.2.9).

3.4.6   Reasoners

Reasoners are applied to the sequent of a given proof tree node and provide a way to contribute to the provers. They are typically of more interest to the developer than the user.

A reasoner is (and has to be) quite "rough" : it takes a given sequent and produces a proof rule that will (if possible) apply to this given sequent. A tactic can use several reasoners by applying them in loops, combining them, or even calling other tactics.

3.4.7 Purging Proofs

Proofs are stored in proof files. Each time a new proof obligation is generated by the tool, a corresponding (initially empty) proof is created. However, proofs are never removed automatically by the Rodin platform. As time passes and a model has been worked out, obsolete proofs (i.e., proofs that do not have a corresponding proof obligation anymore) accumulate and clutter proof files.

The purpose of the proof purger is to allow the user to delete obsolete proofs.

Why proofs become obsolete

Proof obligations are named after the main elements related to it, such as events and invariants. Therefore, each time such an element is renamed manually, the corresponding proof obligations get a new name. However, the existing proof is not renamed, and a new proof gets created with the new name.

Consequently, after a lot of model editing, more and more obsolete proofs are stored in proof files.

Selecting purge input

In any view, right-clicking an Event-B project or file will display a popup menu with a Purge Proofs... option. If several files or projects (or both) are selected, purging will apply to all of them.

Firstly, the proof purger tries to find obsolete proofs in the selection. If no obsolete proofs are found, a message will pop up informing the user that no proof needs to be purged. Otherwise, a new window will pop up displaying a list of all POs that are considered obsolete, i.e. all proofs that exist in some proof file and but no longer correspond to any concrete project or file.

Choosing proofs to delete

For the moment, nothing has been erased. The new window (see Figure 3.51) shows obsolete proofs and allows the user to choose among them and select the ones which should be deleted. One may wish to keep some of them knowing they might be useful in the future.

Once the selection has been decided, hit the Delete button to actually delete the selected proofs from the proof files. Files that become empty will be deleted as well.

Caution

Proof purging should not be performed on models that are not in a stable state. For instance, it should not be applied to a model that has some errors or warnings issued by the type checker. This is because if there are errors and warnings, not all proof obligations are generated. Therefore, some proofs may have been considered wrongly as obsolete.

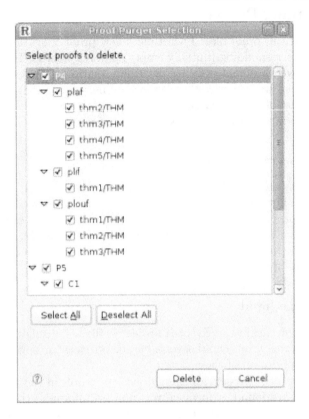

Figure 3.51: Proof Purger Selection Window

3.4.8 Simplifying Proofs

Proofs consists of trees where each node is a proof step. Storing or investigat-
ing a proof consists in saving or reviewing all these nodes. With post tactics
activated, some unneeded steps might be added to the proof, after each manual
step. Indeed, the post tactics try to apply some rewriting and inference rules
which are themselves grouped into proof steps. When the proof step concern
some useless hypotheses, for example, the applied rules are not useful in the
proof. They can even appear cumbersome regarding storage or later investi-
gation of the proofs. Hence, it is recommended to apply simplification before
storage of huge proofs and/or proofs involving extensively post tactics.

Selecting simplification input

In any view, right-clicking an Event-B project or file will display a popup menu
with a Simplify Proof(s) option. If several files or projects (or both) are selected,
simplification will apply to all of them.

Automatic simplification option

It is possible to automatically launch the simplification on proof save. However, because this task can be performance consuming this feature is disabled by default. It can be enabled by selecting Window ⟩ Preferences ⟩ Event-B ⟩ Sequent Prover ⟩ Simplify complete proofs when saving.

Chapter 4

Frequently Asked Questions

4.1 General Questions

4.1.1 Where can I get help?

In addition to this handbook, consider looking in the Rodin Wiki (1.1.2) for an answer.

There is also a vibrant community that is helpful and responsive. You can contact it via the Rodin user mailing list at rodin-b-sharp-user@lists.source-forge.net.

4.1.2 What is Event-B?

Event-B is a formal method for system-level modelling and analysis. Key features of event-B are the use of set theory as a modelling notation, the use of refinement to represent systems at different abstraction levels and the use of mathematical proofs to verify consistency between refinement levels. More details are available at `http://www.event-b.org`.

4.1.3 What is the difference between Event-B and the B method?

Event-B (2.2.4) is derived from the B method. Both notations have the same inventor, and share many common concepts (set-theory, refinement, proof obligations, etc.). However, they are used for quite different purposes. The B method is devoted to the development of *correct by construction* software, while the purpose of Event-B is used to model full systems (including hardware, software and environment of operation).

Event-B and the B method use mathematical languages which are similar but do not match exactly (in particular, operator precedences are different).

4.1.4   What is Rodin?

The **Rodin Platform** is an Eclipse-based IDE for Event-B that provides support for refinement and mathematical proofs. The platform is open source, contributes to the Eclipse framework and can be extended with plugins.

4.1.5   Where does the Rodin name come from?

The Rodin Platform (3.1) was initially developed within the European Commission funded Rodin project (IST-511599), where Rodin is an acronym for "Rigorous Open Development Environment for Complex Systems". Rodin is also the name of a famous French sculptor. One of his most famous works is the Thinker.

4.1.6   Where I can download Rodin?

Rodin is available for download at the Rodin Download page: `http://wiki.event-b.org/index.php/Rodin_Platform_Releases`

4.1.7   How to contribute and develop?

Glad to hear that you want to help! Please see the `http://wiki.event-b.org/index.php/Developer_FAQ` page.

4.1.8   My operating system is not supported! How can I install Rodin on my platform?

At the time of writing this document, prebuild versions exist for only a small number of operating systems. There are two recommended approaches for running Rodin in these situations:

Build Rodin from the sources Users who have some experience in building Java software can simply build Rodin from source. For more information, please consult the Developer Documentation in the Rodin Wiki: `http://wiki.event-b.org/index.php/Rodin_Developer_Support`

Run Rodin in a virtual environment With a fast computer, you can also use a virtual environment (e.g. VirtualBox) and install an operating system into that environment that supports Rodin (e.g. a 32bit version of Linux).

There are other options available for more specialized scenarios (e.g. running 32bit Rodin on a 64bit Linux system). However, the two approaches described above are the most simple.

4.2 General Tool Usage

4.2.1 Do I lose my proofs when I clean a project?

No! This is a common misunderstanding of what a project clean does. A project contains two kinds of files:

- those you can edit: contexts, machines, proofs

- those generated by a project build: proof obligations, proof statuses (each proof obligation is either discharged or not discharged)

The cleaner just undoes what the builder does, i.e. it removes proof obligations and statuses, but it never modifies any proof.

A status may change from *discharged* to *not discharged* when the proof is no longer compatible with the corresponding proof obligation (e.g. when a hypothesis is changed), but **the proof itself is still there!** You can try to replay it.

Confusion may arise when automatic provers have been launched. The cleaner does not undo these automatic proofs (why would it ?!!). Once a proof has been made, the platform does not modify or delete it by itself. Even obsolete proofs are preserved (3.4.7)!

4.2.2 How do I install external plugins without using the Eclipse Update Manager?

Although it is recommended that you install additional plugins into the Rodin platform using the Eclipse Update Manager, this might not always be practical. In this case, you can install these plugins by emulating the operations normally performed by the Update Manager either manually or by using ad-hoc scripts.

The manual installation of plugins is described in *Installing external plugins manually*.

4.2.3 The builder takes too long

Generally, the builder spends most of its time attempting to prove POs. There are basically two ways to shorten this process:

- Disable the automated prover in the Preferences panel.

- Mark a PO as reviewed if you do not want the auto-prover to attempt it anymore.

Note that if you disable the automated prover, you always can run it later on some files by using the contextual menu in the Event-B Explorer.

To disable the automated prover, open Rodin Preferences (menu Window ⟩ Preferences...). In the tree on the left-hand panel, select Event-B ⟩ Sequent

Prover ⟩ Auto/Post-tactic. Then, in the main panel ensure that the checkbox labelled Enable auto-tactic for proving for proving is not selected.

To review a proof obligation, just open it in the interactive prover and then click on the *review* button (this is a round blue button with a *R* in the Proof Control toolbar). The proof obligation should now labelled with the same icon in the Event-B explorer.

4.2.4   What are the ASCII shortcuts for mathematical operators?

A page describing the ASCII shortcuts that can be used for entering mathematical operators can be found in the Help menu. To view this page, select Help ⟩ Help Contents and then select Rodin Keyboard User Guide ⟩ Getting Started ⟩ Special Combos in the window that pops up.

This page is also available in the dynamic help system. The advantage of using dynamic help is that it is able to display the help page side-by-side with the other views and editors. To start the dynamic help, click Help ⟩ Dynamic Help, then select Contents and select the page in the tree.

4.2.5   Pretty Print does not work on Linux

Configuring Rodin on Linux can be tricky. In particular, the pretty print view of the original editor requires an HTML control to render. It it does not work after installing Rodin, you may have to configure xulrunner as follows:

Add a property by appending the following code to your eclipse/eclipse.ini or rodin/rodin.ini file:

```
-Dorg.eclipse.swt.browser.XULRunnerPath=
  /usr/lib/xulrunner/xulrunner-xxx
```

4.2.6   Some mathematical characters are wrong

The Rodin editor must use the correct font to work properly, which is Brave Sans Mono. Depending on the editor, the font has to be configured via Window ⟩ Preferences ⟩ Colors and Fonts ⟩ Basic Text ⟩ Font.

4.2.7   No More Handles

On Windows platforms, Rodin may crash and generate the error message "no more handles". An OS specific limitation is described here and here. A workaround is provided at this site.

4.2.8   Software installation fails

The installation of software from update sites (Help ⟩ Install New Software...) sometimes fails with an error saying something like:

```
No repository found containing:
        osgi.bundle,org.eclipse.emf.compare,1.0.1.v200909161031
No repository found containing:
        osgi.bundle,org.eclipse.emf.compare.diff,1.0.1.v200909161031
...
```

This is an eclipse/p2 bug that is referenced here.
To fix this problem:

- Go to Window ⟩ Preferences ⟩ Install/Update ⟩ Available Software Sites

- Remove all of the sites and then add them back again. This can be achieved in the Available Software Sites preference page by:

  - Selecting all of the update sites (highlighting all those that are checked)
  - Exporting them
  - Removing them
  - Restarting Rodin
  - Going back to the preference page and importing the update sites back (from the previously exported file)

4.2.9 How do I send a bug report?

This depends on the nature of the bug:

- Problems with the core Rodin platform, as well as feature requests, should be filed via the SourceForge bug tracker: `http://wiki.event-b.org/index.php/Bugs_and_Feature_Requests`

- To file problems with individual plugins, check the plugin's documentation in the wiki (1.1.2).

- If you are unsure whether to file a bug or not, consider asking a question on the Rodin user list at rodin-b-sharp-user@lists.sourceforge.net.

- To report a problem with the handbook, use the feedback button that is present in the HTML and Eclipse Help version of the handbook.

4.2.10 Where did the GUI window go?

When you are looking for a particular view, and the view does not appear or if it appears in a different place than is usual, try clicking on Window ⟩ Reset Perspective.... This will reset the different views back to their default positions. If you can't find menu buttons from one of the views, try resizing the view in question to see if part of the menu has been hidden.

4.2.11   Where vs. When: What's going on?

You may have noticed that both in this tutorial, as well as in the tool, events sometimes use the keyword "when" and sometimes "where". The idea of this was to make the formal statements more intuitive. Unfortunately, this created more confusion than anything else.

The short answer is: "when" and "where" in events have exactly the same meaning, for all practical purposes.

The long answer is: In some contexts (but not all), the tool changes the keywords to make the meaning of the event more apparent. The distinguishing factor is the parameter: an event without a parameter uses the keyword "when", and an event with a parameter uses the keyword "where".

To make things even more confusing, this doesn't apply everywhere: The Event-B structural editor always uses the keyword "where", but the pretty print for the Event-B structural editor switches between the two. The default Rodin editor always uses the keyword "where". The Event-B syntax in this handbook has been generated with the LaTeXplugin, which also switches between the two keywords.

4.3   Modelling

4.3.1   Witness for **Xyz** missing. Default witness generated

A parameter has disappeared during a refinement. If this is intentional, add a witness (3.2.4) to tell the machine how the abstract parameter should refined.

4.3.2   Identifier **Xyz** should not occur free in a witness

This means that the Xyz identifier appears in a witness predicate, but Xyz is a disappearing abstract variable or parameter and is not set as the witness label. To resolve this error, set change the witness label to the identifier Xyz.

4.3.3   Witness **Xyz** must be a disappearing abstract variable or parameter in the **INITIALISATION** event

The witness is for the after value of the abstract variable, hence you should use the primed variable. The witness label should be Xyz', and the predicate should refer to Xyz' too.

4.3.4   I've added a witness for **Xyz** but it keeps saying "Identifier **Xyz** has not been defined"

As specified in the Section 3.2.4, the witness must be labelled with the name Xyz of the abstract parameter of the event that is being refined. A concrete example can be found in Section 2.8.5.

4.3.5 How can I create a new Event-B Project?

Please read Section 2.4.2 to learn how to create a new Event-B project.

4.3.6 How can I remove a Event-B Project?

In order to remove a project, first select it on the Project Explorer and then right click with the mouse. The contextual menu will appear on the screen as indicated in Figure 4.1.

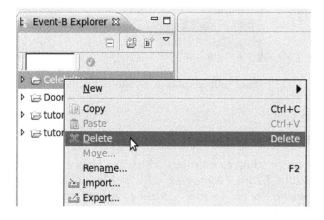

Figure 4.1: Removing a Event-B Project

Simply click on Delete, and your project will be deleted (after you confirm that you want to delete it in the window that pops up). It is then removed from the Project Explorer.

4.3.7 How can I export an Event-B Project?

Exporting a project is the operation by which you can construct automatically a ".zip" file containing the entire project. Such a file can be sent by email. Once received, an exported project can be imported (next section). It then becomes a project like the other ones which were created locally. In order to export a project, select it and then select on File ⟩ Export... from the menubar as indicated in Figure 4.2.

The Export wizard will pop up. In this window, select General ⟩ Archive File and click the Next > button. Specify the path and name of the archive file into which you want to export your project and finally select Finish. This menu sequence (and the various options) is a part of the Eclipse platform. For more information, refer to the Eclipse documentation.

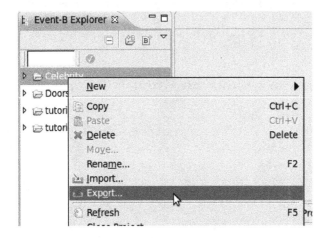

Figure 4.2: Export a Event-B Project

4.3.8   How can I import a Event-B Project?

A ".zip" file corresponding to a project which has been exported elsewhere can be imported locally. In order to do this, click on File ⟩ Import from the menubar. In the import wizard, select General ⟩ Existing Projects into Workspace and click Next >. Then choose the Select archive file option and hit the Browse... button to find the zip file that you want to import. Now click Finish. As with exporting, this menu sequence and layout are part of Eclipse.

   The importation will fail if the name of the imported project (not the name of the file) is the same as the name of an existing local project. This means that when you are exporting a project, it is a good idea to modify its name in case the person who imports the project already has a project with that same name (which could be a previous version of the exported project). Changing the name of a project is explained in the next section.

4.3.9   How can I change the name of a Event-B Project?

Select the project whose name you want to modify, and then click on File ⟩ Rename.... Modify the name and click on OK. The name of your project will then have been modified accordingly.

4.3.10   How can I create a Event-B Component?

Please check Section 2.4.2 to learn how to create a new Event-B component.

4.3.11   How can I remove a Event-B Component?

In order to remove a component, press the right-click on the component. In the context menu, select Delete. This component is removed from the Project

Explorer.

4.3.12 In the new Rodin Editor, how can I add an element to machine?

 Please also consult Section 3.1.4. The editor is described in more detail there.

Whenever you pull up a context menu in the new editor, please pay attention to the following two issues:

- Make sure that the cursor already is on the correct line. If you right-click and the cursor is on the wrong line or in the wrong position within the line, you will get an incorrect context menu.

- Make sure the cursor is not in "edit" mode. This is the case when you are able to edit a textual element. If this is the case, you will also get an incorrect context menu.

The different elements of the machine, can of course, be added using the different wizards for element creation (New Variable Wizard ⚡ , New Variant Wizard ⚡ , New Invariant Wizard ⚡ , and New Event Wizard ⚡) which are described in more detail in Section 3.1.6.

You can also add new elements by placing your cursor directly to the left of the small green arrow (⬦) that appears next to your machine name in MACHINE section. Now right click and select the component that you want to add from the Add Child menu. You can also add an element by right clicking on the heading of the section of the element you want to add (e.g. VARIABLES) and selecting Add Child, or by placing your cursor directly to the left of the small green arrow (⬦) next to the name of any of the components that already exist and selecting Add Sibling. Unfortunately, if your cursor is not directly next to the small green arrow (while the cursor is blinking, the left side of the arrow is actually touching the cursor), these methods do not actually work.

4.3.13 How can I use multiple lines for a comment, predicate or expression (using the new editor)?

To insert a line break while editing any field, use Ctrl-Return.

4.3.14 How can I save a Context or a Machine?

Once a machine or context is (partially) edited, you can save it by using the save button as indicated in Figure 4.3.

Once a "Save" has been completed, three tools are called automatically, these are:

- the Static Checker

Figure 4.3: Save a context or a machine

- the Proof Obligation generator (3.2.7)

- the Auto-Prover (3.1.7)

This can take some time. A "Progress" view can be opened at the bottom right of the screen to see which tools are working (most of the time, it will be the auto-prover). This is done via Window ⟩ Show View ⟩ Progress.

4.4   Proving

4.4.1   Help! Proving is difficult!

Yes, it is. Check out Section 3.4.5 to begin using the provers.

4.4.2   How can I do a Proof by Induction?

This page about proof by induction will give you some starting tips.

4.4.3   What do the labels on the proof tree mean?

- ah means *add hypothesis,*

- eh means rewrite with *equality from hypothesis* from left to right,

- he means rewrite with *equality from hypothesis* from right to left,

- rv tells us that this goal has been manually reviewed (3.1.7),

- sl/ds means *selection/deselection,*

- PP means *discharged by the predicate prover,*

- ML means *discharged by the mono lemma prover*

Index

$\perp$ (false), 138
$\top$ (true), 138
$\wedge$ (conjunction), 138
$\Leftrightarrow$ (equivalence), 138
$\Rightarrow$ (implication), 138
$\neg$ (negation), 138
$\vee$ (disjunction), 138

abstract machine, 123
abstract machine notation, 18
action, 125
addition $(+)$, 151
anticipated, 129
arithmetic, 37
assignment, 125, 153
    become element of $(:\in)$, 154
    become such $(:|)$, 154
    deterministic $(:=)$, 153
    non-deterministic, 154
Atelier B provers, 159
auto prover, 106
auto-tactic, 110, 118
    preferences, 114, 118
axiom, 43, 123
    using a wizard to create an axiom, 96

become element of assignment $(:\in)$, 154
become such assignment $(:|)$, 154
before-after predicate, 126, 154
bijection $(\rightarrowtail\!\!\!\!\rightarrow)$, 149
Boolean
    as type, 35
boolean, 140
    as type, 135
    the operator bool, 140

cardinality (card), 143

carrier set, 35, 122, 135
    using a wizard to create a carrier set, 95
Cartesian product $(\times)$, 145
combinator, 119
comment, 27
component, 25
composition
    backward composition of relations $(\circ)$, 147
    forward composition of relations $(;)$, 147
conjunction $(\wedge)$, 138
consistency of a machine, 127
constant, 43, 123
    using a wizard to create a constant, 96
context, 37, 43, 122
    creation of, 38
    dependencies, 91
    synthesis, 93
convergent, 129

data type, 34, 135
    Boolean, 35
    carrier set, 35
    integer, 35
    user defined, 36
deadlock, 70
derived, 132
discharged, 100
disjunction $(\vee)$, 138
division $(\div)$, 151
domain (dom), 146
domain restriction $(\lhd)$, 146
domain subtraction $(\vartriangleleft\!\!\!-)$, 146

Eclipse, 18, 81

177

editor
    Camille text editor, 26
    default editor, 88
    structural editor, 89
EQL (equality of preserved variable proof
        obligation), 133
equality (=), 139
equivalence (⇔), 138
establishment of the invariant, 127
event, 44, 124
    merging events, 129
    using a wizard to create an event,
        98
Event-B, 18, 167
    explorer, 85
    perspective, 83
exists (∃), 139
exponentation (^), 151
extending
    a context, 122
    an event, 129
extends, 43

false
    as expression (FALSE), 140
    as predicate (⊥), 138
fast view bar, 86
feasibility
    of actions, 127
    of witnesses, 126
FIN (finiteness proof obligation), 133
FIS (feasibility proof obligation), 133
Font, 170
for all (∀), 139
free identifiers, 136
function (↛, →), 149
function application, 150

gluing invariant, 50, 123
goal, 102
GRD (guard-strengthening proof obli-
        gation), 133
guard, 125
    strengthening, 128

identifier, 133

identity relation (id), 148
implication (⇒), 138
import project, 58
proof by induction, 176
initialisation, 45, 127
injection (↣,⤚), 149
integer, 35
    as set (ℤ), 151
    as type, 135
intersection
    generalized intersection (inter), 144
    intersection (∩), 142
    quantified intersection (⋂), 144
INV (invariant proof obligation), 133
invariant, 29, 44, 124
    using a wizard to add an invariant,
        97
inverse (⁻¹), 147

ℒ-operator, 136
lamba expression (λ), 150
live lock, 76

machine, 44, 123
    dependencies, 93
    synthesis, 93
mailing list, 167
maplet (↦), 145
mathematical notation, 32
mathematical symbols, 27
maximum (max), 152
membership (∈), 139
merging events, 129
minimum (min), 152
minus (−), 151
modelling, 172
modulo (mod), 151
MRG (guard-strengthening (merge) pr-
        oof obligation), 133
multiplication (·), 151

NAT (natural number proof obligation),
        133
natural numbers (ℕ), 151
negation (¬), 138
notation

Event-B, 121
    mathematical, 135

oftype operator ($\overset{\circ}{\circ}$), 152
ordinary, 129

pair, 35, 145
    as type, 135
parameter, 29, 125
partition, 143
pending, 100
perspective
    customisation, 86
    Event-B, 83
    proving, 99
plus (+), 151
post-tactic, 110
    preferences, 114
post-tactics, 71
predicate, 33
predicate logic, 17
preferences, 111
    prefix, 112
    profile, 116
    tactics, 114, 118
pretty print, 94
ProB, 30, 42
product
    direct product of relations ($\otimes$), 147
    of integers ($\cdot$), 151
    parallel product of relations ($\|$),
        147
project, 24, 82, 173
    clean, 169
projection (prj_1,prj_2), 148
proof control view, 103
proof obligation, 30
    action feasibility (FIS), 127
    action simulation (SIM), 128
    axiom as theorem (THM), 132
    equality of a preserved variable (EQL),
        128
    generation, 133
    guard as theorem (THM), 132
    guard strengthening (GRD), 128
    invariant as theorem (THM), 132

invariant preservation (INV), 127
    merging events (MRG), 129
    well-definedness of a guard (WD),
        131
    well-definedness of a variant (VWD),
        132
    well-definedness of a witness (WWD),
        132
    well-definedness in an action (WD),
        132
    well-definedness of an axiom (WD),
        131
    well-def. of an invariant (WD),
        131
    witness feasibility (WFIS), 126
ProR Requirements Tool, 23
proving, 57, 156, 176
    perspective, 99
    proof obligation, 44
    proof rule, 156
    proof tactics, 158
    provers, 159
    pruning, 101
    purging, 163
    simplifying, 164
    the proof tree, 100
purging proofs, 163

quantification
    existential ($\exists$), 139
    universal ($\forall$), 139

range (ran), 146
range restriction ($\rhd$), 146
range subtraction ($\rhd\!\!\!-$), 146
reasoner, 162
refinement, 45, 123
    data refinement, 123
    horizontal, 123
    superposition, 123, 129
    vertical, 123
refines, 44
relation, 36
    backward composition ($\circ$), 147
    direct product ($\otimes$), 147
    forward composition ($\circ$), 147

identity (id), 148
image, 148
inverse ($^{-1}$), 147
parallel product ($\|$), 147
relation ($\leftrightarrow, \leftrightarrow\!\!\!\!\!\!-, \leftrightarrow\!\!\!\!\!\!\rightarrow, \leftrightarrow\!\!\!\!\!\!\leftrightarrow$), 145
relational image, 148
reminder, *see* modulo
requirements, 23
reviewed, 100
Rodin, 81, 168
Rodin problems view, 85

sees, 44
selected hypotheses, 102
sequent, 156
set, 43
    as type, 35
    cardinality (card), 143
    comprehension set, 140
    difference set ($\backslash$), 142
    empty set ($\varnothing$), 141
    finite, 143
    operations, 35
    partition, 143
    power set ($\mathbb{P}$), 143
    set extension, 141
    set subtraction ($\backslash$), 142
SIM (simulation proof obligation), 133
simplifying proofs, 164
skip, 128
specification, 23
status of an event, 129
strengthening of a guard, 128
subset ($\subseteq, \subset$), 142
subtraction
    of integers ($-$), 151
    of sets ($\backslash$), 142
superposition refinement, 123
surjection ($\twoheadrightarrow, \twoheadrightarrow$), 149
symbols, 170
Symbols view, 27

tactic combinator, 119
tactics, 158
    auto-tactic, 110, 114
    post-tactic, 110, 114

theorem, 43, 132
THM (theorem proof obligation), 133
traceabililty, 23
true
    as expression (TRUE), 140
    as predicate ($\top$), 138
type, *see* data type
type expression, 135

union
    generalized union, 144
    quantified union ($\bigcup$), 144
    union ($\cup$), 142

VAR (decreasing of variant proof obligation), 133
variable, 44, 124
    common variable, 124
    creating a variable, 26
variant, 129
view
    Proof Control, 103
    Rodin Problems view, 85
    Search Hypotheses, 106
    Symbols View, 85
VWD (well-definedness of variant proof obligation), 133

warnings, 59
WD (well-definedness proof obligation), 133
well-definedness, 136
WFIS (witness feasibility proof obligation), 133
when, 172
where, 172
witness, 47, 52, 126, 172
wizard
    New Axioms Wizard, 96
    New Carrier Sets Wizard, 95
    New Constants Wizard, 96
    New Enumerated Set Wizard, 39, 95
    New Event Wizard, 98
    New Invariants Wizard, 97
    New Variable Wizard, 97

WWD (well-definedness of witness proof
  obligation), 133

xulrunner, 170

yellow highlighting, 28